How to be an Outstanding Primary SENCO

OTHER TITLES FROM BLOOMSBURY EDUCATION

How to be an Outstanding Primary School Teacher, Second Edition
by David Dunn

How to be an Outstanding Primary Middle Leader
by Zoë Paramour

How to be an Outstanding Primary Teaching Assistant
by Emma Davie

Inclusion for Primary School Teachers
by Nancy Gedge

Lesson Planning for Primary School Teachers
by Stephen Lockyer

Practical Behaviour Management for Primary School Teachers
by Tracey Lawrence

How to be an Outstanding Primary SENCO

Jackie Ward

BLOOMSBURY EDUCATION
LONDON OXFORD NEW YORK NEW DELHI SYDNEY

BLOOMSBURY EDUCATION
Bloomsbury Publishing Plc
50 Bedford Square, London, WC1B 3DP, UK

BLOOMSBURY, BLOOMSBURY EDUCATION and the Diana logo are trademarks of Bloomsbury Publishing Plc

First published in 2019 by Bloomsbury Education

A catalogue record for this book is available from the British Library

ISBN: PB: 978-1-4729-6329-1; ePDF: 978-1-4729-6330-7; ePub: 978-1-4729-6328-4

2 4 6 8 10 9 7 5 3

Typeset by Newgen KnowledgeWorks (P) Ltd., Chennai, India
Printed and bound in the UK by CPI Group (UK) Ltd, Croydon, CR0 4YY

Contents

Introduction

What does it mean to be an 'outstanding' SENCO and how can you fit this in alongside all the other commitments you may already have in school? As a former deputy head and SENCO in a primary pupil referral unit who is now working as an independent practitioner in a range of mainstream schools, I can empathise with those at the 'sharp end' of this very demanding but, ultimately, extremely rewarding role. I am currently a SENCO in a number of schools, all of which have had unique difficulties in supporting and retaining previous practitioners; however, the challenges that come with the SENCO role can all be resolved with some forethought and an appreciation of what the job entails. SENCOs who consult with me are invariably trying to do 'too much', which means they struggle to find time to do everything well. Obviously this is self-defeating for schools, staff, children and parents, and I am finding that, increasingly, help is needed to enable the role to be both effective and manageable, without impacting negatively on health and wellbeing.

This book is aimed at would-be, new and experienced SENCOs and takes account of the differing needs and situations of all you wonderful educators who are trying to help the most needy and vulnerable children in our school communities. I recently spent two days with a new SENCO who was also a Year 5 class teacher and was despairing of how to fit the two together successfully; she was overwhelmed by the demands of colleagues and becoming increasingly defeated by the inaccessibility of outside agencies, including county SEND departments, in helping her meet the needs of the pupils. At the end of our time together, during which we reviewed everything she was doing and made some simple changes, she said she was 'empowered' for the first time to move forwards in carrying out this vital role, as she felt that it had been simplified without losing the impact needed for outstanding practice. She also learnt that tenacity is a vital ingredient of the role!

My aim is to cut out extraneous 'paper exercises' and unnecessary procedures (often inherited from previous staff) so that SENCOs have practical, manageable strategies for carrying out their role and feel an increased confidence in explaining this to those to whom they are accountable. As I am a firm believer in giving workable, real-life suggestions, I will incorporate case studies that you may find useful (these are composites from a range of schools, including the PRU I worked in and the mainstream schools I currently work with independently) and suggest 'takeaways' that will help you to develop reflective, knowledge-based practice and extend thinking through further reading and training opportunities.

We can all make a difference to the children in our care if we have a rational, evidence-based approach to supporting their often complex needs. Files, folders and spreadsheets may have their place in demonstrating outcomes, but the real impact comes when our SEND pupils are accessing their learning as happy and confident citizens, moving positively into their futures. I hope you will all find something useful to take away from this book.

Chapter 1
So you want to be, or now are, a SENCO?

We need to consider what the role of the SENCO actually is in school. In this chapter, I will be looking at the 'nuts and bolts' of the job based on a clear understanding of what it entails in terms of core purpose and organisation.

Are you ready to be a SENCO?

If you want to be a SENCO, you must undergo the mandatory SENCO training programme for the national SENCO award (NASENCO) or be enrolled to do so within three years of your SENCO appointment (unless you were already a SENCO prior to the requirements for the qualification, i.e. for at least 12 months before 1 September 2009). Currently, the cost of accessing training from a Nasen-recommended provider is about £2,300 (which needs to be met by your school) but there are also options for online distance learning over the course of a year. For more information, access www.nasen.org.uk/about/partnerships.

This expense means that paying schools will expect a high degree of commitment to the role and you need to be sure that being SENCO is the cornerstone of your future professional development and that you really want to do it. I was recently in a school where the SENCO had left and another staff member – a Year 6 teacher – had agreed to take on the role without knowing the extent of that commitment; eventually, she realised that she only wanted to be a class teacher and, even if given more time, did not want to be away from her class for prolonged periods. She was then able to articulate this to her head (with my support) and started to sleep again at night! It is vital that you come into the post with your eyes wide open before committing to such a key role. Ask around and talk to colleagues in neighbouring schools, speak to national award providers and research extensively online. Social media, such as Twitter, can be a useful source of information and opinion from a range of teachers and specialists; this is very valuable – it's free CPD! Never, ever take on the role because you have been 'asked' without weighing up all the pros and cons. Look at your local education authority (LEA) website to see how supportive they are in terms of special educational needs; they should demonstrate this through their 'Local Offer', which is legally compliant. Also examine the SEND information report on your school website and read the policy. Consider links to the school behaviour policy and whether your school is committed to inclusivity and is prepared to access specialist support when and where necessary. It is no accident that the current SEND regulations (Department for Education, 2014a) recommend that a SENCO should be part of the senior leadership team; it is integral to every school that SEND is at the top of all agendas for school improvement.

I am not trying to discourage would-be SENCOs, as, approached properly, it is one of the best jobs in school – who can resist helping to potentially change the lives of some of our most vulnerable pupils by meeting their needs effectively, and reducing anxiety for parents and colleagues in the process? But it would be foolish of me to gloss over the realities and challenges involved – this is why I am so much in demand as a consultant!

Understanding the SENCO role

When taking on the role of SENCO, or considering applying for the position, it is essential to have a clear understanding of what the role entails. There is a lot of responsibility for ensuring that the assess, plan, do and review (APDR) process is clearly embedded for each child on SEN support through individual education plans (IEPs) and individual behaviour plans (IBPs) set by class teachers (see Chapter 2); the SENCO role also has responsibility for requesting an education, health and care (EHC) needs assessment for children with more complex needs (see Chapter 9).

As a starting point, what does the SEND Code of Practice (Department for Education, 2014a, p. 108) say about the SENCO role?

- 'The SENCO must be a qualified teacher working at the school.'
- 'The SENCO has an important role to play with the headteacher and governing body, in determining the strategic development of SEN policy and provision in the school.'
- 'The SENCO has day-to-day responsibility for the operation of the SEN policy and co-ordination of specific provision made to support individual pupils with SEN, including those who have EHC plans.'
- 'The SENCO provides professional guidance to colleagues and will work closely with staff, parents and other agencies. The SENCO should be aware of the provision in the Local Offer [see Chapter 3, page 28, for further information] and be able to work with professionals providing a support role to families to ensure that pupils with SEN receive appropriate support and high-quality teaching.'

The Code makes a number of further key recommendations about the role of SENCO, including those who may work across a number of small schools, and it is worth a read to recap on the most important points, whether you are just starting out or are a more experienced practitioner. An outstanding SENCO should ensure they have a good grasp of official guidance and not just rely on an individual school's policies and practices; I often find that over-reliance on 'custom and practice' can mitigate against a school's legal obligations to their pupils, as actions may be missed or glossed over. This is why a strategic approach is critical, as the Code of Practice suggests, with actions for children with SEND forward-planned in the context of resources within the budget and those targeted at particular groups, such as pupil premium. You will find that once this is in place and agreed support from the senior leadership of the school has been outlined, it will be much easier for you to carry out your role effectively.

So we have established the top-level objectives of the SENCO role, but what does the day-to-day look like? What are the main duties a SENCO could and should be expected to carry out? The SEND Code of Practice (Department for Education, 2014a, Section 6.90) says responsibilities may include:

- 'overseeing the day-to-day operation of the school's SEN policy
- co-ordinating provision for children with SEN
- liaising with the relevant Designated Teacher where a looked after pupil has SEN
- advising on the graduated approach to providing SEN support
- advising on the deployment of the school's delegated budget and other resources to meet pupils' needs effectively
- liaising with parents of pupils with SEN
- liaising with early years providers, other schools, educational psychologists, health and social care professionals, and independent or voluntary bodies
- being a key point of contact with external agencies, especially the local authority and its support services
- liaising with potential next providers of education to ensure a pupil and their parents are informed about options and a smooth transition is planned
- working with the headteacher and school governors to ensure that the school meets its responsibilities under the Equality Act (2010) with regard to reasonable adjustments and access arrangements [you will need to familiarise yourself with this document before starting the role]
- ensuring that the school keeps the records of all SEN pupils up to date'

I think it is important to note, at this point, that some of the above duties may be held, out of choice, by the headteacher. For example, SENCOs may have a budget for resources but unless you are the head, advising on budget deployment is not usually, in my experience, within the SENCO's sole remit; also, senior leaders and governors may oversee access arrangements, particularly where this is linked to funding. However, I appreciate in some larger schools aspects of these may be delegated to the SENCO.

Also, there is no specific reference to SENCOs having a particular responsibility for assessment arrangements; in section 6.72 of the Code it says that schools should decide their own approach to monitoring and evaluation. I feel this works best as part of a joint approach that is embedded in whole-school tracking systems, as it can be easily linked to other forms of tracking, e.g. pupil premium (we will cover this in more detail in Chapter 10, page 136).

Establishing yourself as a SENCO

When you first agree to become a SENCO, one very important point is to try to establish some ground rules in terms of allocated time to do the job well. Time given can be variable, ranging from 'ad hoc' time for meetings and 'catching up' to dedicated half or full days that are 'ring fenced' for SEND work. The latter is preferable as you can schedule meetings, phone calls, observations and other work into dedicated spaces, which is particularly important if you have teaching or other commitments too! Some SENCOs are worried about time management but are unwilling to approach senior leaders in case they are seen to be 'making a fuss'. Remember, this is a strategic role for the school, and the head and governors have a statutory duty to have a SENCO in place; it is much easier to negotiate time right from the start and then everyone knows where they are in terms of timetabling and action planning. Also, if you are a SENCO with a class, you are less likely to be distracted by what is happening in there if you know cover is regular and secure.

The next important thing is to make sure you have a quiet space to work in, preferably where you can make and take phone calls and hold meetings. I appreciate (working as I do in a variety of settings) that in some schools space can be at a premium, but there should be a corner, at least, that you can call your own, and obviously this is easier to organise if you have a regular slot of time; it is not much fun being 'moved around' by the arrival of phonics or intervention groups! Effective organisation is the key to being an outstanding SEND practitioner (not rocket science, you may think) but often SENCOs who consult with me are extremely disorganised, with paperwork stored in different locations, sometimes in bags, car boots or even at home! Obviously this is not conducive to efficient time management, which is the main issue of concern in many cases.

Problems with storage and equipment can be tricky, I know, but at the minimum, a SENCO should have a computer or laptop that is for their sole use (preferably) and a lockable filing cabinet for files and other papers that is easily accessible, i.e. not at the other end of the school! There should be a space for resources and the use of these will need to be carefully monitored by you as it is easy for items in constant use, e.g. coloured reading overlays, to go 'missing' (a signing-out book is useful). You may well be thinking this is all quite basic common sense, but in the hectic hurly-burly of the day, it is easy to end up 'chasing your tail' if you are having to fly around looking for things; remember, your time is finite!

Top tip

It is worth putting effort into your initial organisation, as this will pay dividends later. If you are 'inheriting' the SENCO role, make time to streamline folders and files, and get rid of anything that is out of date. (SENCOs are notorious hoarders of old National Curriculums, PIVATS folders, etc.)

Record-keeping

In terms of keeping children's SEND records, first acquaint yourself with the new data protection arrangements (Data Protection Act 2018), which came into force in May 2018; all schools will be GDPR compliant now and staff should be trained and have a copy of the applicable regulations in a school policy format.

My preference is to store some class and individual SEND records, for example individual education plans (IEPs), electronically on my computer desktop (password protected) and for each child on the SEND register to also have a cardboard file in which letters and other paperwork can be stored and locked away. Some SENCOs scan everything electronically, but this can have a real downside; firstly it is extremely time-consuming to do and secondly files can get 'lost' or erased. It is wise to ensure that records are simply stored and easily accessible.

Many schools I have worked in have computer folders hidden within folders, hidden on multiple drives that are impossible to locate and keep track of! It is useful if some items, such as provision maps, which are jointly shared by class teachers and SENCOs, are stored on shared drives; the same goes for any blank copies of paperwork that need completing. I always have 'cause for concern' templates available for teachers to complete for a child in their class. This saves time initially until you can arrange an observation or discussion with the teacher. I can remember starting in one school and being followed around by a 'crocodile' of staff wanting to ask me about different children! Reflection time is important before this happens and the form gives you a chance to think in advance.

Planning meetings

Make your diary your friend and make sure you link up any appointments and meetings with the school diary; there is nothing worse than a visitor turning up at school to be met with blank looks from the office staff! It is important to have an overview of the SEND 'timeline' for the year and put in key dates in advance. These can include:

- annual review meetings (EHCPs)
- team around the family (TAF) meetings
- policy and other statutory reviews and website updates
- SEND register updates
- deadlines of any sort, e.g. staff to send you copies of their IEPs and provision maps
- parents' evenings
- meetings with other professionals
- pupil observations and interactions
- specialist teacher reports
- data analysis reviews and meetings with the senior leadership team.

Top tip

Always keep a record of any phone calls made or received and follow up with an email if possible; I often print these out and pop them in the child's file. Even a sticky note signed and dated can be a quick reminder of where you are up to; it does not need to be a lengthy report (you haven't time!).

Effective communication

It is important to keep a chronology of action for every child on the SEND register and ensure any actions are recorded accurately and dated; I keep these on my desktop so I can quickly update them. All class teachers have their own SEND files so I ensure that they receive copies of any letters or other information pertaining to that child and I annotate my file to say I have done so. Again, it sounds simple but I have often had teachers saying to me that they have had nothing passed on, haven't been kept informed and have no idea where they are up to with the child; the key to being outstanding is good communication between all parties! One scenario that sticks in my mind is the teacher who had gone to the previous SENCO to ask about what had happened in a recent TAF meeting and the SENCO told her she did not have the time to tell her! Clearly, this should not be happening and, if it is, warning bells should be ringing! (The SENCO eventually left.)

Good communication is key when dealing with other professionals outside your own setting. I always keep a notebook or diary with the names and contact details of anyone I regularly liaise with. If you are starting from scratch, it is worth taking time to research your key contacts and record their details in advance; these could include:

- Key personnel in your LEA special needs (SEND) department, e.g. educational psychologist (EP), special educational needs and disability officer (SENDO), the name of your school caseworker(s) – they are responsible for collating paperwork, giving clerical support to EPs and SENDOs, and sending correspondence to schools, parents and other professionals.
- Community paediatricians; the first port of call is usually their medical secretaries.
- Speech and language therapy service (SALT).
- Some family doctors, if you are in regular contact.
- Occupational therapists (OTs).

- Children's social care (CSC) where applicable – you may need to liaise with social and family workers.
- Parental support services; your LEA will have a list of relevant contacts.
- Specialist support services for children and parents or families, e.g. support for autistic spectrum condition (ASC) and attention deficit and hyperactive disorder (ADHD), behaviour specialists (these can be found often at local alternative provision or may be independent) and pupil referral services (PRUs).
- Child and adolescent mental health services (CAMHS).
- Child psychology.
- Schools that you link to, e.g. secondary schools; you will be liaising to help a child with SEND make a successful transition from your setting into theirs.
- Early Years providers; you will be working together to provide a smooth transition into your setting for a child with SEND.

As you go along, there will be others you can add to your list, but this is an excellent start, and will save you precious time in the long term.

Top tip

Try to establish, fairly quickly, good working relationships with these professionals. I always make a point of getting to know SEND staff and medical secretaries, asking for them by name (write it in your book!); this is extremely important as they often smooth the way in getting help and support from the senior SEND staff and paediatricians. They will sometimes say, 'I am only the medical secretary', but I usually find they are *the* most important people in passing on information and getting the medical professional to ring you back; ditto SEND receptionists and caseworkers. Once you are all on first-name terms, you can have a little chat and a joke and they will be willing to do anything they can for you! When I left the PRU, I got a signed card from all the SEND staff, hand delivered by the SENDO! Positivity (generally) gets you everywhere!

Case study 1

I have recently supported a school, in a temporary assistant SENCO role, where the environment was not conducive to carrying out the role effectively. There was no designated space or equipment and the role was being undertaken on a temporary basis by a full-time class teacher who was 'helping out' following the promotion of the previous SENCO. Resources were non-existent and pupil files were stored in a faraway part of the school. Space was at a premium and there was no obvious solution. The SENCO was, understandably, feeling rather fraught and was frustrated that she could not do the job properly. She also felt that it was hard to organise meetings or carry out observations and speak with parents as she had no set times to plan for and no regular room to work in – she had to use any available space on the day. My suggested approaches to resolve this difficult situation were:

- There was actually a small room that was used to support pupils in small groups and, if the SENCO had a designated time for the role, instead of it being 'ad hoc', there was flexibility for that room to be available, plus she could take her laptop in with her. Also, there was some storage in there for day-to-day equipment and a phone in the vicinity.
- The files should be stored near to the allocated room to cut out time spent on wasted to-ing and fro-ing.
- Systems should be organised to support the practitioner, and specialists should be brought in to give extra support and contribute to applying for statutory assessment; she should also be given a designated time in the week for SENCO work.

The solutions were simple but when implemented they made a massive difference to that practitioner as she had the time and space to carry out her role effectively. Also, it was good for the school as she was now willing to consider taking on the SENCO work on a long-term basis, and staff and parents knew when she was available to meet with or speak to them.

Chapter takeaways

For time-pressed SENCOs:

- Acquaint (or reacquaint) yourself with the SEND Code of Practice (Department for Education, 2014a), focusing on Section 6 for schools and Section 5 if your school is also an Early Years provider.
- Familiarise yourself with the Equalities Act 2010.

For time-rich SENCOs (or relatively so!):

- Dip into other relevant sections of the Code of Practice and reflect on your own practice in line with your school's policies and national legislation.

Chapter 2
Now what do you need to do?

The 'nuts and bolts' are in place – you have a secure understanding of the SENCO role and you have the space, time and personal organisation to undertake it effectively – so it is now the time to have a more detailed look at next steps for creating an agreed response to a child's individual needs, with close reference to the Code of Practice (introduced in Chapter 1). The starting point for this is to look at the school SEND register.

Reviewing the SEND register

Whether you are a new SENCO or an existing one, it is important to regularly review the SEND register and ensure that all children with additional needs are included; the SEND Code of Practice (Department for Education, 2014a), Section 6.14 onwards, says:

> 'All schools should have a clear approach to identifying and responding to SEN... a pupil has SEN where their learning difficulty or disability calls for special educational provision, namely provision different from or additional to that normally available to pupils of the same age.'

The issue I find many SENCOs have is that they feel they are expected to provide specific strategies and guidance to teachers in the form of individualised support plans or provision maps. I have worked in schools where the SENCO was writing individual education plans by themselves and handing them out to teachers! In one school the SENCO was writing out detailed guidance for every teacher on specific SEN, e.g. ASC, ADHD, linked to individual children whilst running her own class more or less full time. As a result, the class teachers were adding more and more children to the register, exacerbating her already unreasonable workload!

It is quite clear in the SEND Code of Practice Sections 1 and 6 that quality-first teaching is key to addressing special educational needs in the first instance. In 1.24, it states: 'High quality teaching that is differentiated and personalised [underpins] special educational provision... and is compromised by anything less.' In section 6.37, it says: 'Additional intervention and support cannot compensate for a lack of good quality teaching.' Initially, therefore, it is the class teacher who should be planning and differentiating for children with possible SEN and ensuring that every child has access to quality-first teaching. There are many debates about children being 'velcroed' to the sides of support staff, but the main issue is that children with SEN should have direct input from the class teacher; the teaching assistant is there to support this process as part of a carefully formulated joint approach. Neither is it the responsibility of the SENCO to put programmes in place for individual children and provide detailed plans; their responsibility is to manage the process of further support, e.g. engaging a specialist teacher, referring cases on to relevant professionals, medical or otherwise, and seeking help and support from the LEA SEND department.

In order to be an effective and outstanding SENCO you need to ensure that you are not doing other people's jobs for them, otherwise you will become 'bogged' down and of no help to anybody. One school I have worked in, under a previous head, 'collected' children with SEND (including those with challenging behaviours) into one class and had the SENCO and deputy teaching them 'en masse'; you can imagine how that turned out! Fortunately, with the advent of 'quality-first teaching', class teachers are rightly asked to have ownership of the needs of their children rather than having the children 'farmed out'.

However, it is reasonable for class teachers to ask for SENCO help when they have tried a number of strategies that don't appear to be effective and they are unsure of what to try next. This is where it is useful to have a planned response that is shared with all staff in school, so that they know how to proceed. Suggested ideas are:

- Having procedures in place for identifying underlying needs, for example the 'cause for concern' templates I discussed on page 9.
- Having a summary sheet that outlines different areas of need and what you might see; I use an absolutely brilliant resource aimed at class teachers that comes courtesy of an amazing educator, Chris Chivers, available at https://chrischiversthinks.weebly.com/blog-thinking-aloud/send-2014-possible-class-teacher-crib-sheet; Chris is happy for his resources to be used as long as he is credited, and I have used it widely!
- Providing advice on when to put in an intervention. There are existing templates such as the 'Wave 1–3' interventions, where Wave 1 is quality-first teaching and Waves 2 and 3 are small group support moving to personalised learning for more complex needs; however, I feel it is more important to focus on needs-based learning that fits into your particular setting – many schools already have their own programmes of interventions for reading, phonics, spelling and maths, so it is pointless to try to introduce separate systems.
- Providing useful links to websites that give more information on the areas of need, e.g. ASC, ADHD, speech, language and communication difficulties (see Chapter 7, page 83, for suggested examples).
- Supplying templates for IEPs; it is important that these are standardised across the school.
- Having a policy on how and when to have conversations with parents about initial concerns – this is important in large primaries; in smaller settings the class teacher and I discuss the best way forward. Often I have that discussion once it is decided that the child should be on the SEND register, and parents usually appreciate this.
- For the SENCO to observe the child before advising on next steps. (This is why eliminating unnecessary workload is so vital, as it is the children who are top priority.)

Top tip

It is important to clarify with senior leadership which systems they agree should be in place, otherwise the whole thing can fall apart. My most proactive headteachers reinforce these through INSET and staff meetings with realistic deadlines, e.g. for submitting IEPs; staff soon get on board with these and they become part of the expected school procedures.

Developing a whole-school approach

Having robust school systems in place, with all staff having a clear picture of their roles and responsibilities, means that procedures are more effective and help for children with SEND can be targeted at an early stage. There has to be a whole-school approach to making decisions about what should be done and when, where and how; this should be linked to demonstrating what the Code of Practice calls a 'graduated approach' to assessing need and planning next steps. Section 6.36 of the Code clearly states that:

> 'Teachers are *responsible and accountable* [my italics] for the progress and development of the pupils in their class, including where pupils access support from teaching assistants or specialist staff.'

However, it is unreasonable (in my opinion) for schools to 'enforce' time-consuming paperwork on already overstretched class teachers, striving to meet the needs of 30-plus pupils! Where this does happen (and sadly it does!), managing SEN becomes a box-ticking paper exercise, which does little to address practical support for the child. As SENCO, it is your responsibility to try to ensure that systems are as simple and streamlined as possible; SENCOs I advise are often expecting too much recording of a child's difficulties, which can duplicate the work already being done. There are many examples of what the graduated approach should look like, for example from SEND professionals, LEAs and SEND organisations, but I will stay with the official guidance outlined in the Code of Practice, Section 6.44, as this is statutory:

> 'Where a pupil is identified as having SEN, schools should take action to remove barriers to learning and put effective special

education provision in place. [This] should take the form of a four-part cycle through which earlier decisions and actions are revisited, refined and revised with a growing understanding of the pupil's needs and of what supports the pupil in making good progress and securing good outcomes.'

The four stages of the approach recommended by the Code of Practice are 'assess, plan, do, review', and the SENCO and class teacher will liaise together at each stage of the process, known overall as 'SEN support'. Let's take a look at this in more detail.

Assess

A cause for concern form is filled out by the teacher and passed to the SENCO. There is a possible discussion with parents as part of the process or when a need has been identified (it could be the SENCO who has that discussion); either way, schools have a duty to inform parents at this stage.

The pupil is added to the SEND register, with parental agreement; it must be clear that a child has additional needs, over and above those that can normally be met in a classroom situation through appropriate differentiation. This needs careful consideration, taking into account teacher assessment and experience, previous progress and attainment, and parental and pupil views. If specialists or other professionals from health and social care are involved, their views should be taken into account in informing assessments. If other professionals are not involved, the SENCO should consider contacting them or referring in to them as appropriate, with parental agreement. It is important to note that you should keep chronologies of action for all children on your register (some will have more on than others, depending on their level of need, e.g. additional medical needs). These chronologies will inform your APDR, so it is useful to include some measure of impact or next steps rather than just listing dates of actions – I have an extra column for this and I keep the files on my computer desktop so that I can easily edit them. If you are applying for an EHCP, chronologies will need to be included in the paperwork.

At this point you should already be deciding which professionals you need to consult with. If a child has language and communication need, SALT are the appropriate service. If there is a suspected underlying learning or medical need, e.g. ASC or ADHD, a referral to the local paediatric services should be made; I have never yet found this to be time-wasting as families benefit from speaking to a range of professionals about their child's needs and schools also feel supported in planning next steps. Many health trusts have a one-stop system so that you can refer in to a range of professionals, which is very useful and makes the tracking of appointments much simpler.

Plan

Once SEN support has been agreed, all parties should discuss what needs to be put in place – adjustments, support and interventions – with a clear review date. Schools will have a format for recording this, such as individual education plans, learning plans and pupil passports, and any interventions should be recorded on provision maps.

Provision maps can come in many forms but need to be right for your setting, fitting in with existing school assessment and recording systems; however, it needs to be clear what interventions the child is receiving, and impact needs to be part of the monitoring process. I will address provision maps in more detail in Chapter 10, page 138.

Do

The class teacher is responsible for working daily with the child and overseeing any one-to-one or group interventions with support or specialist staff. You, as SENCO, will support the class teacher in assessing the progress of this work and making further suggestions or provision to help the child.

Review

Support and interventions should be reviewed in line with the agreed date in terms of pupil progress and further changes made if these are not effective. At this point, it may be useful to consult with an educational psychologist who can observe and assess the child and make further recommendations. It may be at this point (usually after two cycles of intervention, which allows for 'tweaking' and getting further help) that an application for statutory assessment towards obtaining an Education, Health and Care Plan is considered. Your LEA SEND department will expect to see evidence that clear provision has been made under the graduated approach.

The important thing is that you can evidence to parents and other professionals that everything is being done that can possibly be done to help meet a child's needs and 'break down' their barriers to learning.

Top tip

As part of this process, it is worth getting expert advice about a child where possible; as well as helping the child, this will contribute to your continuing professional development (CPD) as SENCO, as you will be engaging in a professional dialogue that may add to your understanding of particular conditions or difficulties. There are often SENCO support groups run by your LEA, private providers and accredited trainers who will help 'keep you up to speed' on the latest developments and findings. This 'topping up' of expertise is what will make you outstanding in your field. Obviously, this will need to be tailored to your other commitments.

More information can be found on the graduated response at Nasen (www.nasen.org.uk/resources/resources.sen-support-and-the-graduated-approach-inclusive-practice.html); Nasen are a membership charity organisation supporting educational professionals and it is well worth your school becoming a member if they are not already. Guidance on IEPs and provision maps can be found on a number of SEND forums but Nasen SEND Gateway shares school examples of effective provision mapping (www.sendgateway.org.uk/resources.provision-map.html). Both Nasen and Nasen SEND Gateway have useful resources, articles and other publications to support SEND and SENCOs in school; these include examples of IEPs and other similar documentation. I would advise asking around local schools and SEND professionals if you are wanting to change your format; one I am currently using has the 'assess, plan, do, review' cycle in-built, which teachers are finding really useful as it evidences the graduated response and can easily be evaluated. However, it is all about finding a format that works for you and is easy to manage.

Next steps

So what do you need to be thinking about for next steps? Let's recap:

- Identify, in conjunction with the class teacher, who should be on SEN support.
- Follow 'assess, plan, do, review'.
- Look at procedures for assessing needs and putting interventions in place.
- Liaise with parents and other professionals, and gain a pupil view too where possible.
- Consider appropriate paperwork and procedures, ensuring that SEN support is effective but not too onerous for either class teachers or yourself; make sure that these are fit for purpose.
- Ensure that procedures and school systems are clear and well supported by senior management, including the headteacher.
- Facilitate the easy accessibility of relevant paperwork, e.g. on shared drives.
- Try to avoid complex, box-ticking systems of accountability that mitigate against practicality and add to workload.
- Liaise with appropriate educational and medical professionals to support the needs of the child.
- Check that interventions put in place are effective, as per assess, plan, do, review (see above).
- Have regular progress reviews with parents for children on the SEN register (this can tie in usefully with parents' evenings) and for those on EHCPs (see Chapter 9) in line with the Code of Practice.
- Update chronologies regularly and link to the graduated response (see above and then Chapter 9 for relevance to EHCPs).
- Check that the pupils meet the criteria for SEND; one school I worked in had children who were able, gifted and talented (with no underlying needs) on the SEND register! They also had

IEPs for all children in receipt of pupil premium, regardless of SEN need. The Year 6 teacher submitted 32 IEPs, which was obviously unsustainable (and inappropriate)!

Top tip

Class teachers can demonstrate initial evidence towards potential SEND through annotated planning; they should not be asked to repeat this separately. An IEP or other document should be linked to SMART targets (specific, manageable, achievable, relevant and timely). I have spent a lot of time in meetings demonstrating this to staff, and the key is to make sure that targets will move a child forward as soon as possible – small steps are important!

Case study 2

One school I advised was struggling to collect evidence towards submissions for EHCPs; their SENCO had recently left and there were a number of children at various stages of SEN support. I was asked to act as temporary SENCO to unpick what was happening and to review procedures and practices in general. Now, at this point it feels very much like being a detective; you have to follow the clues and find the missing pieces. Usually you have to go back to the beginning to unravel chronologies, discovering in the process what has happened or not happened.

Some of the issues were organisational, i.e. there was missing paperwork, no proper chronologies, no orderly systems of filing and desktop storage, and not much evidence of what the school had put in place for the child. There was a child's folder with paperwork for an EHCP that had been turned down by the authority, but nothing to indicate why – the letter sent out to the school was missing. An examination of other files told a similar story; crucial documentation was missing. There was no evidence in any of them of what steps were being taken to meet the child's needs; chronologies were mainly lists of actions, such as medical appointments and meetings, with no actions arising or evaluations of impact. There were no copies of IEPs, either in the files or on the desktop; in short, there was no evidence of a graduated response.

Now this is not SENCO shaming – there were some complex reasons behind a high SENCO turnover in that particular school – but it proves my point about having good systems in place, specialist help and adequate release time for the job to be done properly. Completing the SENCO award, sadly, does not prepare you fully for the practical day-to-day role, as many SENCOs have said to me; it is a whole-school responsibility to make SEND support work.

These are (some of) the actions I undertook in this school over a period of time:

- Organised the files and desktop so that all relevant information was to hand.
- Updated chronologies, adding next steps and evaluations of impact.
- Chased up appointments and put in referrals to medical and other professionals, e.g. SALT, paediatric service (some children needed re-referring).
- Made to-do lists for the most urgent cases; these were the pupils in great need of an EHCP to support their complex needs.
- Undertook some staff training on what a graduated response should look like, linked to quality-first teaching and accountability.
- Re-jigged the IEPs to include the 'assess, plan, do, review' cycle.
- Reviewed the SEND register with the headteacher and eliminated children who were not needing SEND support, e.g. able, gifted and talented (AGT) pupils who had no underlying issues such as social and communication difficulties, and those on pupil premium with no additional needs.
- Standardised provision mapping across the school.
- Standardised protocols and procedures with the support of the headteacher.
- Brought in some more resources to support the teaching and learning of children with specific SEND needs.
- Enlisted the support of EPs, SENDOs, paediatricians (through their medical secretaries), CAMHS and behaviour support agencies in helping to meet individual needs.
- Updated records and ensured that missing documentation was tracked down and stored in relevant files.
- Made sure that all teachers and other staff had copies of paperwork relevant to them and were kept fully informed.

Obviously, this was a big job as we had to start from scratch, more or less, but it highlights the value of being well organised and having an effective whole-school approach. The head is now considering appointing a SENCO who will carry out the role part-time, without linking it to a class teaching role; in a school with such complex levels of need, I think this is the right approach.

Chapter takeaways

- Familiarise yourself with the graduated response, looking at the SEND Code of Practice 2014, and think about relevant paperwork, e.g. IEPs.
- Do some extra reading around graduated response and useful documents, e.g. IEPs, provision maps. Consider which fit most appropriately with the school setting and have the most impact. Tweak school systems as appropriate, based on a reasoned response, in conjunction with the senior leadership of your school.

Chapter 3
Legal requirements and duties

In order to be an outstanding SENCO, it is vital to have an understanding of the legal requirements that underpin the SEND regulations, so in this chapter I am going to pull together all relevant legislation and signpost you to relevant, useful organisations for further guidance and support. I will also include information on school website requirements and SEND policies.

Legal requirements

For an overview of the legal requirements relating to SEND provision in schools, the key document to start with is the SEND Code of Practice (Department for Education, 2014a); the introduction to the Code outlines all relevant legislation and lists those who must have regard to the guidance, including local authorities, governing bodies of schools, proprietors of academies, management committees of PRUs and Early Years providers. It states that 'where the text uses the word "must" it refers to a statutory requirement under primary legislation, regulations or case law' (Section i). The guidance refers to Part 3 of the Children and Families Act 2014, the Equality Act 2010 and associated regulations.

Children and Families Act 2014

It is helpful to have an overview of this Act, and to inform yourself it is useful to refer to 'The young person's guide to the Children and Families

Act 2014' (Department for Education, 2014b), which gives information in an easily readable format. This guide describes the purpose of the Local Offer, for example, saying: 'Under the Act, every local council in England must write down what help there is in their area for children… with special educational needs or a disability.' (p. 23)

The key points of the Children and Families Act 2014 are:

- For councils to ensure that education, health and social care services work together.
- For councils to ensure that children and parents are given information about their SEND.
- For councils to ensure that children with SEND and their families know where to go to get help.
- For councils to make sure that organisations work together to help children with SEND.
- For children with SEND and their parents to have more say in what help they get.
- For there to be one overall assessment of need (EHCP) and for a school, young person or parent to be able to ask the council for this to be carried out.
- For the EHCP to run from birth to age 25 and be reviewed annually.
- For there to be an option for families to choose some of the help they get in the form of a 'personal budget' (see Chapter 9, page 125, for more information).
- For there to be procedures in place for children or parents needing to appeal about provision, including having mediators and going to tribunals.

Your council website should have all the relevant information pertaining to the requirements of the above Act on its 'Local Offer' page, including links to outside agencies, such as independent support specialists for parents (they are trained in all legal aspects pertaining to SEND and schools). For more information, read Section 4 in the Code of Practice; other linked legislation includes The Special Educational Needs and Disability Regulations 2014 (Part 4; UK Government, 2014a).

Top tip

It is worth familiarising yourself with what is on the council 'Local Offer' page, as it gives useful information for parents on local support groups and activities as well as step-by-step guidance for parents and schools on applying for statutory assessment (including the referral paperwork) and appealing against SEND decisions. I usually pass this information to SEND parents (often via the school newsletter) so that they are aware of their entitlements and what is available in the local area.

The Equality Act 2010

All schools have a duty to children with SEND under the Equality Act 2010. Section 6.9 of the Code of Practice says:

> 'All schools have duties under the Equality Act 2010 towards individual disabled children and young people. They must make reasonable adjustments, including the provision of auxiliary aids and services for disabled children, to prevent them being put at a substantial disadvantage.'

The introduction to the Code of Practice (pages 16 and 17) gives more detail on discrimination and the distinction between children with a disability, for example a long-term health condition, such as asthma, and those with a disability and SEN whose needs fall under the remit of SEN planning and review. The latter are covered under both SEN and equality legislation. Governing bodies have a statutory duty to publish access arrangements for disabled children and the steps taken to prevent them being treated less favourably than other children.

What does this mean for schools?

The impact of these regulations on schools usually centres around an application for statutory assessment. Guidance for this process can be found on your local authority website as part of their Local Offer, but confusion can arise when trying to unpick all the steps needed in making an application for an EHCP (see Chapter 9, page 115). In addition, the Code of Practice, Section 4.32, sets out the full requirements necessary in the Local Offer for educational, health and care provision.

The local authority must outline all provision for SEN for children in the area from relevant education providers – this includes funding arrangements and the use of delegated budgets. It includes the arrangements providers have in place for:

- identifying SEN
- consulting with parents of children with SEN
- getting help for children with SEN, including appropriate services and having the right provision and equipment in place
- supporting transition arrangements between settings for children with SEN.

The Local Offer must also give information on:

- teaching approaches, additional support for SEND, adaptations and reasonable adjustments
- outlining available facilities for children with SEND
- assessing and reviewing the progress of pupils with SEND
- securing professional expertise to support children with SEND, including relevant continuing professional development (CPD)
- assessing local authority effectiveness in the provision it offers for pupils with SEND
- available activities for children with SEND, including extra-curricular and physical activities
- pastoral and emotional health and wellbeing support for children with SEND
- including and making provision for children with SEND who are looked after by the authority.

Throughout, there is an emphasis on joint working practices between health, education and social care, and this underpins statutory assessment.

As a SENCO, it is worth being aware of what a council's legal requirements are, as there can be disagreements between schools, parents and SEND departments with regard to the rights of, and provision for, children with SEND. The best way forward is to know what the law says and take the correct course of action by engaging positively with the right professionals to sort any problems out.

In addition, it is important to know that schools are required to pass on information about pupils with SEND to the local authority, and this is done via the School Census; this information is used to inform strategic SEND planning and contributes to the national SEN information report.

The school website

Schools are required to publish more detailed information about identifying, assessing and providing for pupils with SEND and this needs to be displayed prominently on the school website in the form of a SEN information report. Further information on this can be found in the Code of Practice under 'Publishing information: SEN information report' (Sections 6.79–6.83). The governing bodies of maintained schools and academies are responsible for this and the information must be updated annually. Information is taken from the Special Educational Needs and Disability Regulations 2014 and must include:

- types of SEND and relevant policies for identification of these
- in mainstream schools, the name and contact details of the SENCO
- arrangements for consulting parents about their child's SEND and involving them in the child's education
- how children with SEND are consulted and involved within school
- assessment and review procedures
- transition arrangements
- teaching and learning approaches for pupils with SEND
- adaptations and adjustments within the learning environment and in the delivery of the curriculum to pupils with SEND
- staff training and expertise and provision of specialist support
- evaluation of the effectiveness of school provision
- the provision of support for a pupil's social and emotional welfare needs

- how the school interacts and engages with other professionals, including health and social care and the local authority
- the inclusion of children with SEND in activities undertaken by children who do not have SEND
- arrangements for handling parental complaints about school provision for children with SEND
- looked after children.

The local authority will usually have a model template covering the above information, which can be personalised to the school. As all schools have to publish this on their websites, there is also an opportunity for you to ask your local authority for a variety that exemplify best practice. The report must link to the local authority's Local Offer page and must be displayed prominently on the website. It must be set out in clear and unambiguous language. It should include information about the school SEN policy (see below) and contain all relevant contact details.

Top tip

It is worth pausing here to say that the amount of legislation attached to educating pupils with SEND can seem quite daunting, and the responsibilities attached to being SENCO can be overwhelming; however, there is support out there if you are unsure. In my experience, headteachers often take responsibility for drafting or co-drafting the SEN information report as it could be open to legal challenge if not completed correctly; also, Ofsted will focus on this when checking that a school website is legally compliant. The key is to work collaboratively with senior leaders when drafting what is, in essence, a legal document.

The SEN policy

So what is the purpose of the SEN policy and what should it contain? Whilst the SEN information report is written from the perspective of children and parents, the SEN policy explains how the school will meet its statutory duties and link to other relevant policies and guidance. Again, your LEA should have guidance on this linked to statutory requirements, in the form of an editable template, and you should ask your LEA SEND adviser for examples of model policies. The policy will include:

- a statement of the school's beliefs and values about SEN
- links to the SEND information report, SEND Code of Practice, Equality Policy and other relevant school policies
- contact details for the SENCO and SEND governor
- aims and objectives
- information about the identification of SEND and links to quality-first teaching
- information about areas of need (see Chapter 5, page 64)
- details of the graduated approach
- information about monitoring and evaluation
- details of the support offered to families
- admission and transition arrangements
- links with other agencies
- how the school supports pupils with medical conditions
- details of resources (including funding) available at the school
- roles and responsibilities in the school relevant to SEN
- how the school stores information (under the Data Protection Act 2018)
- the school's accessibility plan
- a policy review
- how the school deals with complaints
- how the school deals with bullying (with links to behaviour and safeguarding policies).

Top tip

It is worth having a checklist ready when updating an existing policy. It is also useful if you can review the policy with your school SEND governor as it gives them some ownership of what is a statutory responsibility for the school.

Ofsted requirements

As already stated, Ofsted will be looking at the school website to see whether it is legally compliant, so it is worth mentioning here what Ofsted will expect to see during a school inspection. The 'School inspection handbook' (Ofsted, 2015, Section 198) says:

> 'Inspectors will consider the progress of pupils who have special educational needs and/or disabilities in relation to the progress of all pupils nationally with similar starting points. Inspectors will examine the impact of funded support for them on removing any differences in progress and attainment. The expectation is that the identification of special educational needs leads to additional or different arrangements being made and a consequent improvement in progress.'

Ofsted will therefore be evaluating your school in light of the progress and outcomes children with SEND are making, and there are a number of judgements across the Ofsted framework criteria that will reflect this.

An interesting article on this, 'Can OFSTED be a SENCO's best friend?', by renowned SEND expert Brian Lamb (2018), can be found on Real Training and is helpful in terms of highlighting what Ofsted will want to know from the school in addition to information published on the website. The senior leadership team need to be clear on progress being made by learners with SEND, underpinned by robust assessment procedures (see Chapter 10, page 133), and class teachers should be able to demonstrate the steps being taken to support learning under 'assess, plan, do and review' (see page 19). If a child has an EHCP, teaching and learning objectives should be closely linked to the plan recommendations via an IEP or learning plan.

Top tip

It is worth considering the introduction of 'pupil passports', as these involve the child contributing to his or her own learning by showing an understanding of their learning needs. In an Ofsted inspection, it is powerful if a child can have that conversation with an inspector and, in my opinion, this trumps any amount of data that the school produces (important though that is). The website www.pupilpassport.co.uk explains the benefits of having these in place for children with SEND. Although there is no legal requirement to use pupil passports, parental and pupil voices are a vital component of statutory duties in SEND, and a one-page profile, which all contribute to, shows that all voices are heard equally and respected. The website gives links to templates to use or adapt; I have found the one on Twinkl (I know many teachers use this website but bear in mind it is a subscription service) to be very user-friendly.

Upholding legal requirements in day-to-day practice

Once you are confident that you understand the legal aspects of SEND and know where to go for help, it is crucial to ensure that your day-to-day practice enshrines the relevant legislation. Relationships are key to this process, ensuring that all lines of communication are kept open between the school, pupils, parents and relevant outside agencies. One way forward is through the CAF – TAF or CAF – EHA process.

CAFs, TAFs and EHAs

A CAF or common assessment framework is a tool for identifying and assessing a child's needs, planning next steps and engaging relevant professionals to support those needs. Parental consent is needed to open one, with a 'lead professional' appointed to initiate the process, and information is then stored by the school and the local authority; copies are given to parents and shared with the professionals involved.

The CAF process is supported by regular TAF or team around the family meetings where all parties gather together to decide on next steps, which again are recorded and shared; actions are decided on collaboratively and contributions are shared out equally. The CAF – TAF process should support assess, plan do, review (see page 19) and ensure that all avenues are explored in getting the right support for the child and family, including independent support groups and external agencies. Some authorities have EHAs (early help assessments) instead of CAFS, but these do the same job in facilitating co-ordinated, multi-agency support.

Further information on CAFs, TAFs and EHAs can be found on your LEA website via the Local Offer.

Supporting parents

There are a number of independent supporters for parents who need further help in getting the right education for their SEND children, which they are entitled to under the law, for example support in making legal challenges and going to tribunals. The Local Offer page on your LEA website will signpost you in the first instance to independent advice and support services (IAS) and it is useful to make parents aware of this at an early stage, particularly if you are applying for an EHCP. The website Council for Disabled Children hosts the Information, Advice and Support Services (IASS) Network (at https://councilfordisabledchildren.org.uk/information-advice-and-support-services-network), which is a national network supporting local IAS Services (formerly known as Parent Partnership) across England. The IASS Network is funded by the Department for Education and is based within the Council for Disabled Children in the National Children's Bureau. They:

- 'Promote the development and standards of IAS Services.
- Provide training to IAS Services on a range of subjects including the law... (with IPSEA [see below]).
- Promote service impartiality and arrangements that ensure IAS Services operate at "arm's length" from their local authority.
- Provide a national picture of the work of IAS Services through annual reporting.' (Tower Hamlets Council, 2018)

The Council also provides a resources and help hub, which signposts young people, parents and professionals to training and support.

The IPSEA or Independent Parental Special Educational Advice (www.ipsea.org.uk) offers independent legally based advice, support and training, including dispute resolution with schools and LEAs and formal complaint procedures. Along with the Council for Disabled Children, they provide training to IAS Services across England.

Special Needs Jungle (www.specialneedsjungle.com) is a parent-led information and resources site concerning children and young people with SEND; they present numerous updates on government policies and advice and also publish a number of parent-led articles and opinion pieces on SEND.

Case study 3

A parent whose child was in receipt of an EHCP felt that he was now really struggling to access mainstream provision, as he was presenting with extreme anxiety and in tears every day about coming to school, despite having a differentiated curriculum and high one-to-one support; the parent felt that specialist school provision would be more appropriate to meeting his needs. The class teacher and I, as SENCO, liaised to ensure that all targets in his EHCP were being met and that everything was being done that could be done to reduce his anxiety levels, by boosting his self-esteem and encouraging him to feel he was being the best that he could be. Unfortunately, his parent felt that nothing more could be done (she was not blaming the school) and we called an early statement review to discuss next steps; part of the process included visiting a local special school. The SENDO attended the review, as did the educational psychologist (EP), and the following was agreed:

- The EP would come and observe and interact with the child.
- The SENCO (me) would provide updated paperwork, reviewing EHCP targets and progress made.
- The special school we visited would send a staff member to observe and provide an action plan.

The outcomes were:

- The EP felt that the child was making small steps of progress, as did the staff member from the special school.
- My updated paperwork also showed small steps of progress were being made, but focused on the emotional toll taken on the child, who struggled to access learning without almost constant one-to-one support above and beyond that which was funded through the EHCP, and included his inability to cope in wider school life.
- The paperwork was seen by two senior LEA SEND managers, who turned down the application for a special school as, on paper, the pupil was making progress; however, this did not take into account the wishes of the parent or the child's increasing distress in attending school.

Now I am not going here into any 'rights or wrongs' as perceived by interested parties and wish to focus on what I could realistically have achieved as SENCO. I facilitated the access to local IAS Services and they advised the parent on what to do next. It is important, as SENCO, to relinquish, at this stage, further responsibility for appeal 'next steps' and focus on what the school can usefully facilitate to support the child and parent further. In my case, this included:

- Liaising with the next teacher to put in place an induction programme to 'settle' the child in and offer reassurance; fortunately, the teacher already had a positive relationship with him forged in transition visits.
- Moving a familiar support staff member with him to his new class.
- Advising the parent to avoid a negative discussion involving the 'move up' and to try to ensure that the summer holiday was free of stress relating to this, and that the child was able to relax fully. (They planned a lovely trip.)
- Advising the parent to try to ensure that the return to school was relaxed and to communicate positivity about the new class.
- Monitoring closely the transition to the new class and liaising positively with the parent and child.

The SENDO advised me that if the above did not work we could hold a further review meeting and discuss a way forward; in the meantime, the IAS would be able to advise the parent appropriately.

When the autumn term came, the child moved successfully into his Year 3 class and established good relationships with new staff and peers. Transition arrangements worked well and I met with mum to seek her views on how he was coping from her perspective. Mum said he was back to his happy, smiley self and was finding the work easy! (What this means in practice is that he had carefully chosen tasks that were fostering a little independence and promoting small steps of progress.) This is not to say he was not getting this before – the change was that mum was herself less anxious and was much more positive with her child, hence he was not picking up on her 'stress'. We agreed to monitor his progress but so far, so good!

Chapter takeaways

- Familiarise yourself with relevant legislation and your LEA's Local Offer, in conjunction with your school's SEN information report and SEN policy.
- Familiarise yourself with the relevant parent support services outlined above and find out what information could usefully support you in your role as SENCO.

Chapter 4
Supporting children

Many times I am asked by SENCOs (including experienced ones) which children should be added to the SEND register and what support should be offered; this is because, in the main, it can sometimes be unclear whether the child in question needs additional and different support other than that which can be provided in class under the remit of 'quality-first teaching'. I have spent many hours observing children to support SENCO and class teacher judgements; the difficulties arise when deciding whether provision is differentiated sufficiently in class in order to give the child the best possible chance to succeed.

Unfortunately, not all teachers are able to identify which children in their class need to have that different provision and the pupils may be given work that is too hard for them; also there may well be insufficient support staff within a class to support the teacher in meeting individual needs. Yes, quality-first teaching is vital, but without some extra help, it is extremely difficult for the teacher to meet the needs of all children on their own.

So how can we identify the children with additional needs? The summary sheet (via Chris Chivers) mentioned in Chapter 2 is useful for class teachers in identifying a variety of needs. In the next sections, I will set out the main areas of difficulty and outline what you might see in school; this information should be considered during the assess phase of ADPR. I will group them under the four areas of need (as per the Code of Practice):

- Communication and interaction
- Cognition and learning

- Physical/sensory needs
- SEMH (social, emotional and mental health).

Communication and interaction

Speech, language and communication needs

Nasen, the special needs charity (www.nasen.org.uk), published a report from a Nasen Leadership Conference in February 2016, which focused on supporting pupils with speech, language and communication needs (SLCN). I recommend you read this report as it links theory and practice with useful examples that can be incorporated into quality-first teaching.

The signs that a child may have SLCN are:

- struggling with literacy
- possible behaviour issues
- low self-esteem
- limited play
- struggling with social interactions
- poor working memory.

Nasen (2016) say 'Evidenced and impactful intervention for SLCN should follow a graduated approach', including 'communication supportive classrooms' with schools auditing resources, strategies and materials, 'targeted support' with 'evidenced interventions for some children', and 'specialist support'. This final point is vital as it empowers teachers by giving suitable strategies to support the pupil. If you feel a child has SLCN needs, you could:

- Talk to the parents: They may already have concerns about their child at home, for example struggles with reading and homework and interactions with friends or family, or may not realise the problems their child is experiencing in school.
- Talk to the child: Children may welcome the chance to tell you what they are finding difficult in school – it might be they

find it hard to talk to adults or their peers, have struggles with friendships, or have difficulties in reading or writing.

- Recommend a paediatric/SALT referral: Parents can do this via their family doctor; in some areas, schools can refer in directly with parental permission. It is useful to check out whether there are any underlying medical needs, and SALT can help unpick communication difficulties.
- Consider reasonable adjustments: The child may need their work to be suitably differentiated; they may need overlearning (see the Chapter 7 section on precision teaching); they may need visual cues to support learning; they may need to pre-learn new vocabulary or new topics; they may benefit from taught or modelled skills in social communication, friendships or managing anger, or interventions in phonics, reading and writing.

There are a number of organisations that specialise in speech, language and communication needs. NAPLIC is a charity of professionals supporting language and communication development and they champion research into SLCN. Links to a number of further organisations can be found on the NAPLIC website at naplic.org.uk. There is also a fabulous organisation called The Communication Trust (TCT). Their website, www.thecommunicationtrust.org.uk, has a wealth of resources for children, parents and professionals (including initial teacher training providers and students) and CPD short courses to enhance practice across the age ranges. TCT is a coalition of over 50 not-for-profit organisations working to support SLCN. The cover page provides invaluable links to:

- identifying SLCN
- the Speech, Language and Communication Framework (SLCF; a free online professional development tool)
- What Works (the biggest database for speech, language and communication interventions)
- a video on talking to parents.

There are a host of other resources that supplement SLCN advice in schools, but always consider the need for formal referrals to county SALT provision; if you are not sure, contact your local centre for further advice – I find that speech and language therapists are happy to help and, if requested, will often come into school to observe a child and give strategies and materials to the class teacher (this is usually after a referral has been accepted).

Case study 4

A child was being monitored for SLCN at SEN support but on moving to a Key Stage 2 class started to really struggle, despite an individualised curriculum, support from a specialist teacher and a referral to a paediatrician. The paediatrician felt there was a family history of SLCN and diagnosed global developmental delay; I felt that attention deficit disorder (ADD) might be a factor as she displayed some characteristics (without hyperactivity). The symptoms (linked to inattentiveness) are outlined on the NHS website and these include:

- 'having a short attention span and being easily distracted
- making careless mistakes – for example, in schoolwork
- appearing forgetful or losing things
- being unable to stick to tasks that are tedious or time-consuming
- appearing to be unable to listen to or carry out instructions
- constantly changing activity or task
- having difficulty organising tasks' (NHS, 2018).

The pupil showed the above characteristics to a marked degree and also had issues with working memory; despite high one-to-one support from the class teacher and classroom support staff, she was unable to retain even simple information and there was a lot of 'overlearning' taking place. The child had one close friendship in the class but there was a high degree of dependency from her on the other child and if that friend was not available, she displayed high anxiety and seemed 'at a loss' without him. Other coping strategies included asking frequently to go to the toilet and taking a long time to complete simple known tasks; also she would 'hide away' when the class were asked questions, although she would sometimes put her hand up, hoping not to be asked, but to look 'the same' as the other children.

After a lot of discussion in school, I consulted with the link educational psychologist (EP) and we agreed certain strategies to follow:

- use of precision teaching (see Chapter 7, page 87)

- use of visual cues and prompts
- use of pre-teaching skills (see Chapter 7, page 87).

These were put in place with limited success (even though they were linked to specialist teacher advice) and the EP agreed to come in and observe the child and speak to parents; we hoped the outcomes would be linked to providing evidence for an EHCP application.

When the EP saw the child and talked to parents, staff and the specialist teacher, we all agreed that the child needed high one-to-one support to make even small steps of progress. It was agreed that the specialist teacher would work with the child on building small steps of independence in carrying out simple activities linked to the curriculum and the school would carry on with any strategies that proved successful, however small the steps of progress might be. As SENCO, I am now awaiting the EP's report and then I will be liaising with the SENDO in relation to the next steps in applying for statutory assessment. The child is also now seeing our in-house SALT professional to develop her social communication. However, the main objective is to reduce the child's anxiety and give helpful strategies to the class teacher on managing this, so I am spending time in class to do just that.

Top tip

There will be other children in the class or the school with SLCN, and it may be that the children can be supported in small groups for specific SLCN interventions. In one of my schools, the county SALT person came to observe a child but was then able to discuss with the class teacher a number of other children who would benefit from the recommended strategies; the teacher, an NQT, felt hugely supported and was able to put these strategies into place straight away. There are a number of interventions that can be used and I will discuss these in Chapter 7.

Cognition and learning

Children may struggle to achieve age-related expectations in the core subjects of maths and English for a number of reasons. These may include:

- Specific learning difficulties (SpLD), which can encompass a range of conditions such as dyslexia, dyspraxia and dyscalculia; I will look at strategies to address these in Chapter 7, page 85.
- Issues with working memory. They may take the form of poor retention or a struggle to access strategies for learning in a consistent way; there are no quick fixes, but see Chapter 7, page 87, for possible ideas to support this.

Physical/sensory issues

Physical needs

Children with physical disabilities are usually well supported by external services such as occupational therapy (OT), paediatrics, SALT and other medical services. It is important to ensure that children have what they need, e.g. good wheelchair access, physical aids and appropriate specialist support. As SENCO, it is important that you keep a record of specialist equipment and visits from professionals to ensure that special chairs, wheelchairs, splints, etc. are properly checked, especially if the child has a growth spurt that means the size or height of equipment needs adjustment. It is vital to also check with your SEND department about the need for an EHC needs assessment and ask an educational psychologist to assess whether there are any learning as well as physical needs; physical needs may be a barrier to learning but additional adult support is often required to facilitate safe handling procedures, e.g. in and out of chairs or to the toilet. A risk assessment will need to be in place to support this. (Contact a medical professional overseeing the child to check what needs to be included to keep the child and adults safe; your LA SEND or specialist teacher service may be able to provide advice and training – this will usually have to be bought in by the school, as it is often part of a traded service.) Liaise with parents on a regular basis – they are experts in their child's care – and ensure that you are working together to support the needs of the child in the best way you can. Above all, get the views of the child! They may be really struggling with a piece of equipment – a child in one school had just had splints fitted to his legs, which were too tight. It took a while for adults to realise what the problem was!

Case study 5

I was working in a school in a SEND capacity and preparing for a child's annual review; he was disabled and in a wheelchair. In discussion with staff, we found there were all kinds of useful technology resources that would help him in the classroom but that had not been thought of; we even found money for a new laptop and accessed more appropriate specialist teacher support. The annual review process (see page 81) is an opportunity to review provision and update resources that best meet the child's needs.

Hearing impaired (HI) or visually impaired (VI) children will be in the care of medical and other professionals; however, if there are any concerns that a child is struggling to see or hear, ask parents to take their child to the family doctor for a referral to an audiologist or take them for an eye test; it sounds common sense, but these things do get missed! The National Deaf Children's Society (www.ndcs.org.uk) has a wealth of resources and information for schools and families in supporting a deaf child. Similarly, RNIB (www.rnib.org.uk) has information to support visually impaired pupils and their families. Teachers for HI/VI children are usually part of the LEA specialist teacher service and they will check equipment, e.g. hearing aids; train staff in managing the child's needs (for example, there may be someone on the staff who would be willing to learn sign language if that would help); or suggest suitable strategies to help with accessing the curriculum. Communicate regularly with the child and parents/carers to ensure that their needs are being appropriately met.

Case study 6

A school I was working in discovered that one of their children was profoundly deaf after years of hearing tests, grommets (tiny tubes inserted into the eardrum that help clear blockages) and SALT engagement; hearing aids were prescribed and the pupil had to get used to wearing them. We enlisted staff training from a deafness specialist and accessed some additional specialist teaching to support day to day. The LA was contacted with regard to obtaining an EHC needs assessment as there were also significant gaps in the child's learning and high adult one-to-one support was needed.

Sensory processing disorder (SPD)

Although SPD can be found in children on the autistic spectrum (see below), it is also a stand-alone disorder where the brain and nervous system have trouble processing or integrating stimuli (for more information, see autismawarenesscentre.com). SPD is a neurophysiological condition in which sensory input – from either the environment or one's body – is not well detected or interpreted and leads to either hypersensitivity (overstimulation) or hyposensitivity (craving stimulation).

A child with SPD may:

- exhibit behavioural problems
- struggle to calm after being upset
- refuse to eat certain foods due to textures or taste
- be hypersensitive to certain clothes or fabrics or need weighted clothing
- like or dislike being dirty
- be hyper or hyposensitive to loud sounds or smells
- have an odd posture
- present as being dyspraxic
- have delayed fine or gross motor control
- constantly be on the move
- display signs of anxiety
- have a fear of crowds.

You may also need to consider sensory issues such as pica (this is where a child who is hyposensitive to touch, i.e. craves the feel of something, may put a range of objects in their mouth, some of which may not be safe).

So what are the next steps?

- Talk to the parents: They may already have concerns about the child's behaviour at home or may not realise the problems their child is experiencing in school.
- Talk to the child: Many children are aware that they are struggling in a large group, often due to sensory overload, e.g. loud sounds.

- Recommend a paediatric/OT referral: Parents can do this via the family doctor or, in some areas, schools can refer in directly with parental permission.
- Consider reasonable adjustments: Facilitate the use of chewy toys and ear defenders to meet sensory needs. If children struggle in a noisy dining hall or have food issues, they may be better in a small group if that can be facilitated. Many schools I go into have a 'lunch bunch' club, and this nurturing environment can help reduce stress; it is also useful for children who are anxious in the playground due to their sensory needs.

As a SENCO you can assess sensory needs in a range of children by working with a parent to complete a simple sensory questionnaire; there is a useful checklist by Developmental Pathways for Kids at www.developmentalpathways.com/services-sensory.html. This is not about diagnosing anything – occupational therapy services have the expertise to do this – rather it is about looking at triggers for certain behaviours and putting in strategies to manage this. Training is available from a range of providers, but I have had valuable input from Becky Lyddon (www.sensoryspectacle.co.uk), who also provides great workshops for parents. Her immersive workshops contain installations that replicate sensory experiences felt by a child with SPD.

SEMH

Autistic spectrum disorder (ASD) or condition (ASC)

The National Autistic Society (2016) say autism is:

> 'a lifelong developmental disability that affects how people perceive the world and interact with others. Autistic people see, hear and feel the world differently to other people. If you are autistic, you are autistic for life; autism is not an illness or disease and cannot be "cured" [...] Autism is a spectrum condition. All autistic people share certain difficulties, but being autistic will affect them in different ways.'

It is important not to have a stereotypical view of what you think autism 'looks like'; I have had teachers and SENCOs say to me 'Child X is not autistic because he relates well to others, does not present with sensory issues, can empathise.' However, if you look at the checklist of possible signs below, you should be able to see some patterns emerging, of which anxiety is usually key.

In December 2012, the Department for Education published a report entitled 'SLCN pupils: how their needs change as they progress in school'. One of the statistics (p. 4) was: '3% of seven year olds (Year 2) have been identified as having [SLCN], whilst 0.8% have been identified as having [ASD].' This shows the link between both conditions, but the main issue, for me, is whether there is any proper diagnosis of either of these. I have found, as I have travelled around, that there are inconsistencies in the way paediatric services and SALT operate, even within the same county! Some professionals will take referrals and follow them up, whilst others will argue that they cannot see a child as he or she does not fit the criteria in their opinion! However, there is no 'best fit' for ASD; each child is an individual with strengths and difficulties unique to them, and this can pose a problem.

Some 'naughty' children displaying challenging behaviours are actually often having sensory 'meltdowns' due to sensory overload, and then there are 'calm' children who clearly show 'traits' but may present few obvious difficulties in class. However, what characterises both these groups is underlying anxiety and a difficulty in making sense of their environment. The process of gaining an ASD diagnosis is complex, involving a multi-disciplinary approach from a number of professionals, including paediatricians, SALT and a social and communication panel, who look at all the gathered evidence to reach a decision. However, even if there is no diagnosis, the signs are:

- The child may not respond to his or her name or appears not to hear you at times (although you should check their hearing in the first instance).
- The child avoids being cuddled or held, and seems to prefer playing alone, retreating into their own world.
- The child avoids making eye contact and lacks facial expression.

- The child does not speak or has delayed speech, or loses previous ability to say words or sentences.
- The child cannot start a conversation or keep one going, or only starts one to make requests or label items.
- The child may speak with an abnormal tone and may use a singsong voice or robot-like speech (often this can take the form of an 'American' accent!).
- The child may repeat words or phrases but doesn't understand how to use them.
- The child struggles to understand simple questions or directions.
- The child does not show emotions or feelings and may lack empathy.
- The child has difficulty recognising non-verbal cues, such as interpreting other people's facial expressions or body postures.
- Often, the child may have obvious sensory issues around loud noises, food and touch and may exhibit body signs such as hand flapping (stimming) or rocking, which they use to self-soothe.

So, what can you do if you feel a pupil is possibly on the spectrum? First of all, it is worth reiterating that not every child with ASC needs any additional support in school; many can cope well in a school setting and just need keeping an eye on in case anything changes. If there are some difficulties, you could:

- Talk to the parents: They may already have concerns about their child at home or may not realise the problems their child is experiencing in school.
- Talk to the child: Many children are aware that they are struggling in a large group, often due to sensory overload, e.g. loud sounds. Some children will say they worry a lot when their routines are changed or they may be fixated on what to us seem like minor issues, but to them are really huge; there may be a lot of hidden anxieties that need unpicking.
- Recommend a paediatric/SALT referral: Parents can do this via their family doctor or, in some areas, schools can refer in directly

with parental permission. The child will need referring into SALT as they are key in establishing social and communication difficulties and it is their report that goes to the social and communication panel that considers a diagnosis of ASC.

- Consider reasonable adjustments: Facilitate the use of chewy toys and ear defenders to meet any sensory needs or the use of an individual workstation to aid concentration. Visual timetables can help scaffold the day and signpost when things are going to change. If children struggle in a noisy dining hall or have food issues, they may be better in a small group if that can be facilitated. Many schools I go into have playtime/lunchtime clubs, often run by a family support worker or learning mentor, and this nurturing environment can help reduce stress; it is also useful for children who are anxious in the playground and need a safe space.

Case study 7

I work with a number of children with SEMH as a specialist teacher, and one eight-year-old pupil, who displays many of the features of ASC, although he has no diagnosis as yet, was concerning his school as he was presenting with high anxiety levels in a number of situations. The main issues were:

- He worried about other children 'looking' at him and thought they were whispering about him.
- He was constantly pointing out small marks and scratches on his arms and legs and could tell you how he had got each of them, showing obvious concern.
- He worried that his friends might find out 'secrets' about him (for example, taking his teddy to bed) and then laugh at him.
- He would recount minor incidents that had happened in school weeks ago and get upset about them.
- In class, he would often appear to be in his own little world and found it hard to concentrate on his work or listen to what the teacher was saying.

I was able to discuss his worries with him and come up with a plan of action to help him. This was:

- To put all his 'old' worries in a box, seal it and throw it away (this worked immediately!).
- To engage with the relaxation book *When My Worries Get Too Big* (Dunn Buron, 2013), which has really good teaching activities linked in; these also focus on what the child does really well, and I learnt that my pupil was a fantastic rapper, story writer and model maker! (This is so important to raise self-esteem.)
- For his teacher or teaching assistant to ensure that he had some 'reasonable adjustments', such as prompts at times where the class was having direct instruction and support with individual learning to get him started and ensure he could complete tasks independently.
- For his mum to continue with the 'worry box' at home so that he wasn't dwelling too much on what had happened at school.
- To focus on the 'five point scale', which teaches pre-emptive strategies for managing worry before it gets to 'five', which is extreme anxiety (this is at the back of *When My Worries Get Too Big*); we discussed strategies for calming down and pre-empting anxiety, for example deep breathing, doing something nice (making a model), removing yourself from an uncomfortable situation and seeking help from an adult.
- Sharing the scale and calming strategies with home (there is a sheet that can be printed off).

A really excellent resource that I can thoroughly recommend for SENCOs and teachers is Lynn McCann's (2016) book *How to Support Pupils with Autism Spectrum Condition in Primary School.* It is chock-full of practical advice and strategies that really work! She also has a book of social stories, *Stories That Explain* (McCann, 2018), which are great for ASD children as they focus on one small area of difficulty with social and communication skills and give simple strategies for the child to use.

Lynn has a consultancy, Reachout ASC, and her website has lots of really useful free resources and ideas; Lynn works with children across the county and is highly valued by our schools. She also hosts training events across the country. If you haven't got in-house expertise, it can be worth buying in a specialist for advice as it may save money and stress for the school in the long term and the child (and parent) will be getting the right help and support.

Case study 8

I have a child in one of my schools who has had behavioural problems in the past that we now know are linked to ADHD (for which he is now being medicated), possible ASD (this is being looked into) and an SPD (hypersensitivity) linked to noise, touch, taste and smell. I have found it incredibly useful to sit down with his parent and complete a sensory questionnaire to pinpoint exactly where his difficulties lie; it has set up a useful dialogue, which has also helped the parent, about how we can further support the child in school and at home by having an increased awareness and understanding of his difficulties. The child now has ear defenders for certain times of the day and there is a reasonable adjustment for him kicking his shoes off when he is working in class, as long as it does not distract him or others. The parent is implementing similar strategies at home so that there is consistency of approach across the board. As a result, the child is calmer and more settled and is accessing learning very positively and making good progress.

Attention deficit hyperactivity disorder (ADHD) or attention deficit disorder (ADD)

There are many myths surrounding ADHD, including that it is not 'real' or that it is just down to poor parenting or poor diet (although these things may exacerbate the condition). However, the ADHD Foundation (2012) say: 'ADHD is a lifelong condition… the latest research in the *Lancet* medical journal suggests that it is actually a genetic condition.' This research involved a study of the brains of children with ADHD, which revealed that they develop in a different way to those of children without it.

I am finding as I go into different schools that there is a wider acceptance of ADHD as a genuine condition or disability, but the difficulties lie in getting parents on board – many worry about possible medication – and in obtaining an actual diagnosis via the community paediatrician.

So what are the signs and symptoms of ADHD and ADD?

- Low concentration levels: An inability to concentrate or focus on any given task for more than a few minutes (although this can be misleading – in my experience a child with ADHD can concentrate for long periods on a self-chosen activity, such as a favoured computer game!).

- Extreme impulsivity: Many times a teacher will comment on a child 'telling lies' about something they have done, even when seen doing it, but it is typical of that 'spur of the moment' reaction to avoid getting into trouble! You may see a similar reaction when a child 'hits out' at another child for no apparent reason.
- Extreme restlessness: Often the pupil will be fidgety and constantly moving; this is particularly noticeable at carpet times or when a child is required to listen quietly.
- Social and communication difficulties: A child with ADHD may find it difficult to interact positively with others or follow adult instructions, rules and boundaries.
- Inattentiveness without hyperactivity: Some children may display extreme inattentiveness but not the hyperactivity or impulsivity and they may therefore have ADD; these pupils often get missed as they do not display the behaviour issues often associated with ADHD.

There is a wealth of information to be found on the ADHD Foundation website (www.adhdfoundation.org.uk) and www.adders.org.

If you suspect a pupil has possible ADD or ADHD, what steps can you take?

- Talk to the parents: They may already have concerns about the child's behaviour at home or may not realise the problems their child is experiencing in school.
- Talk to the child: Many children are aware that they are struggling to focus or concentrate. I have known children to become very emotional or upset when they struggle with self-regulation and genuinely are unaware of their negative behaviour and how it affects others.
- Recommend a paediatric referral: Parents can do this via the family doctor or, in some areas, schools can refer in directly with parental permission.

- Consider reasonable adjustments: Look at, for example, fiddle toys, an individual workstation (to avoid distraction of self and others) or short, focused activities. Try 'now and next', where 'now' is a directed task and 'next' is a self-chosen box of activities to be accessed independently by the child when they have completed the task. Sometimes a timer can help, although this may be distracting, so caution is needed.
- Advise pre-emptive strategies: When a child becomes restless, offer them an opportunity to access physical exercise or 'take a message' to another class.
- Structure playtimes and lunchtimes: A child with ADHD will struggle at unstructured times and may be disruptive. Structured outdoor or indoor activities and buddy or mentor systems are beneficial for the pupil and the school and prevent flashpoints developing.
- Recognise a child's strengths: A child with ADHD can be extremely creative and think fast. Comedians are a case in point – many have ADHD. See Zoë Kessler's (2011) blog 'Class clown: why are ADHDers so damn funny?' for an interesting read. It is easy to focus on the negatives rather than the pluses!

Medication is often a thorny issue for parents; because ADHD is 'invisible', parents can be resistant to the prescription of stimulants, often because they don't want to medicate their child and feel it may be harmful. However, for children at the extreme end, who are in danger of exclusion, medication can be life-changing, in a good way. I always advise parents to discuss this carefully with the community paediatrician and point them in the direction of any local ADHD parent support groups (see your LEA Local Offer page for links).

Case study 9

When I was at the PRU I taught a young boy (aged six years) who was on respite from his mainstream school due to his hyperactivity and extreme impulsivity, and was in danger of permanent exclusion for hitting out at others. It was fairly obvious from the start that there was an underlying issue and that he did not mean to hurt other children but struggled to self-regulate in certain situations, particularly unstructured times such as playtimes. His over-boisterous behaviour meant that he had real problems with social communication and was becoming isolated from his peers. He had good family support and his older sibling did not present with any issues; his parents were in despair. Eventually he was referred to community paediatrics and received a diagnosis of ADHD. Mum tried to control the symptoms with a rigorously healthy diet with, sadly, limited effect. In the meantime we found another mainstream school to take him but his parents did not want to try medication; the placement began to break down due to his behaviour and his parents reluctantly reconsidered and trialled him on meds. A few months later, we received an email from mum to say he was like a different child; he was doing really well in his learning, had made a lot of friends and was a key member of the football team – all things he could not do before successfully. This is not an advert for medicating per se but in this case it turned a life around, which was spiralling down at a young age.

Case study 10

I was in a school where a young man aged nine years with impulsive and violent behaviours was in imminent danger of permanent exclusion. I referred him to community paediatrics, where he got a diagnosis of ADHD, and collated paperwork for a successful application for statutory assessment. The school got some support from an alternative provision provider who placed him in their setting for a short period; he also started on medication. The most moving thing was when he said to his mum that 'the helicopter in my head has stopped spinning'; this just goes to show what a negative effect ADHD can have on the child. He has returned to his mainstream school now and, with support funded partly by his EHCP, is managing to access learning calmly and improve social communication with his peers and teachers.

I need to stress here that there is no magic wand for ADHD or ADD but that appropriate strategies *can* be utilised successfully!

Attachment issues

The Simply Psychology website (www.simplypsychology.org/bowlby.html; McLeod, 2017) gives an easy-to-read précis of John Bowlby's 'evolutionary theory of attachment', which 'suggests that children come into the world biologically pre-programmed to form attachments with others, because this will help them to survive'. The key figure, according to Bowlby, is the mother, and if this attachment is not secure, then this can have a lasting impact on the child's future relationships.

This is a complex area and I recommend you research further or speak to a specialist in this field as it can be tricky to unpick. Children who are fostered or adopted may display attachment issues, but these can also be found in families with an absent parent or poorly formed relationships with a primary caregiver. More information for schools and parents can be found on www.attachmentdisorder.co.uk. Attachment signs can mimic the signs of ASC, ADHD and SPD and children will benefit from strategies found in Chapter 7 for these conditions. It should be borne in mind that attachment issues arise from early trauma and are informed by ACEs (adverse childhood experiences). It is worth contacting your SEND office or looking at the Local Offer on the LEA website to see whether training is being offered in this area. In my own county, experienced child psychologists attached to the LEA offer a range of free training to schools as part of their brief on supporting mental health and wellbeing. Children with attachment issues will often require personalised learning programmes, as poor emotional health can impact on learning. They need firm rules and boundaries but may not be emotionally in a place to access rewards or sanctions, so these need a personalised approach. A trusted adult is key for poorly attached children, although it may take time to build a relationship; however, it is important to recognise that change is difficult for the child and they will often test boundaries as they may think the adult is going to leave them. This is particularly the case for CLA (child looked after), who may have had a number of foster carers. If the child is CLA, contact the LEA Virtual School for support; often high-needs funding is available to provide extra adult one-to-one support or therapy, e.g. play therapy. There are no 'quick fixes' for children with attachment issues and they require long-term nurturing support in order to form secure attachments. If the child requires an EHC needs assessment, contact the SEND office for advice and, if possible, speak to your school/LEA educational psychologist for help with resources; in some authorities, the educational psychologist can offer training to schools on attachment issues.

Top tip

It is worth bookmarking or noting down any useful websites or resources as and when you find them. You could link to the four areas of need; this will save time as you will have them at your fingertips when needed.

Chapter takeaways

- Focus on the communication aspect of SLCN and explore the resources available on relevant websites, e.g. Nasen and The Communication Trust (TCT).
- Look at the National Autistic Society, the ADHD Foundation and adders.org to upskill yourself on these conditions and plan interventions for pupils in your school.

Chapter 5
Supporting colleagues

There is an emphasis in the SEND Code of Practice (Department for Education, 2014a) on the statutory duty of teachers in relation to quality-first teaching and this is also covered in the Teachers' Standards (Department for Education, 2011; Standard 8). It is a whole-school responsibility to ensure that teachers are meeting that standard, and support will come from the senior leadership team. Once this is embedded then you, as SENCO, should not be asked to carry out unnecessary tasks or actions that are actually the class teacher's responsibility. It is well worth looking at the Nasen website and reading the 2015 download on 'High quality teaching' (Browning, 2015); it clearly sets out the duties and responsibilities of the class teacher, with really useful advice on the deployment of teaching assistants and some great infographics showing support pathways. I would advise all colleagues to use this to reflect on their own practice, but it would be invaluable for newly qualified staff in particular.

When the teacher has done their part, then you can step in with further help. The most important way of supporting colleagues is to ensure that you have sufficient time to:

- Go into classes and observe what is happening (in my experience there is no substitute for this).
- Talk to them and discuss solution-focused strategies and ways forward.
- Ensure that help and advice is practical and doable.

- Talk to pupils and parents to further unpick issues and problems.
- Take action to provide or signpost further support.
- Make available suitable resources (ensure you have a specific budget for SEND).
- Signpost training opportunities (this is why it is vital to work closely with the SMT as they need to support where possible).
- Consult with specialist medical services or other professionals.
- Keep colleagues informed so that they know what is happening (this can get 'lost' in a busy day).

Regular class visits

Outstanding practice is about having a detailed knowledge of the needs of all children and potential children on your SEND register and making regular visits to classes to find out how they are getting on and whether further support is needed. It is easy to wait for staff to come to you, but sometimes, because they are so busy, it does not happen right away. I find that if there is a real problem, with challenging behaviour for instance, you know about it right away, but the quiet child who may be struggling with cognition and learning can be 'missed' for a while because they are not posing an immediate problem. Often these only get flagged up properly in Year 2 and above, when it is clear that the child is below age-related expectations; the pressures of SATs and other tests mean that this is red-flagged.

Many SENCOs say to me that they do not get time to go into classes or work with individual children; in my opinion they are not effective in the role if that is the case – often this role becomes a box-ticking, pen-pushing job with an onus on paperwork and often a pressure to 'get' an EHCP! Again, this needs to be taken up with senior leaders (and is why the Code of Practice says that SENCOs should be part of the senior leadership team); it is like asking a class teacher to assess pupil progress without teaching the child first! Good hands-on practice and good paperwork are inextricably linked – without evidence of quality-first teaching and a robust graduated response, it is impossible to demonstrate how a child has been adequately supported; if an EHCP is required then that evidence is absolutely vital.

So how can this be made to work, even if in less-than-ideal conditions? Again, it is about embedding routines and planning your time carefully. In one of my roles, I have had one day per week in a primary school with a high proportion of SEND children. Once I had organised the practicalities, as outlined in Chapter 1, page 7, I set up a routine for the day:

- Before school starts I visit each class for a quick chat so that any problems can be raised immediately.
- At the same time, I take round copies of any relevant post or paperwork received; I always annotate files to say I have done this.
- If any teacher wants me to look at a child, I establish a time for doing so (not necessarily on that day) so that the teacher feels supported and it is not left 'up in the air'.
- I make a point of 'catching up' with the head as soon as I can in the day so that pressing matters are addressed, concerns raised and an action planned. (In a bigger school this may be another member of the SLT.)
- If I have arranged to go into a class, I make sure that I enable or put in place something that is helpful to the teacher and the child.
- If a specialist teacher is seeing a child, I ensure that advice is shared after each session with relevant staff; I work closely with my specialist teacher and we always allow time to discuss progress and next steps in line with a solid graduated response. This is particularly important if evidence is being collated towards an application for an EHCP.
- All meetings, for example TAF meetings, are co-ordinated for that day and if staff cannot attend, I make sure that I have an update from them and outcomes are reported back as soon as possible. (Remember the poor SENCO in Chapter 1, page 10, who said she 'did not have time' to feed back to the teacher?)

Consistent support procedures

I was recently asked to run a 'SENCO day' for a large multi-academy trust (MAT), which was both a privilege and a challenge. SENCOs are such busy people with huge extra demands placed upon them, and I wanted it to be relevant and useful. There was to be a mixture of new and experienced practitioners, which added to the challenge, as it is hard to not be seen as 'condescending' or just plain boring to those with a wealth of expertise in the role. However, one piece of advice that was well received by all was to do with paring down practice in a seamless manner.

In many schools I work in, I have introduced procedures that mirror each other from classroom practice to SENCO to whole school; at the heart of this is the graduated response, 'assess, plan, do, review', covering the four areas of need:

- cognition and learning
- SEMH
- communication and interaction
- sensory and physical needs.

This system can be replicated through:

- IEPs that have the four areas of need and 'assess, plan, do, review' as headings for SMART targets. Staff say this is a much clearer format for them to focus on and later evaluate. It is also easy to see cycles of progress and plan next steps.
- 'Assess, plan, do, review' SENCO templates that chronicle actions, next steps and outcomes.
- CAFs and TAFs using the 'assess, plan, do, review' headings for actions by parents, the school and other professionals.
- Whole-school monitoring of SEND in an 'assess, plan, do, review' format.

Top tip

Often schools will have a myriad of IEPs, provision maps, waved interventions, tick lists and monitoring sheets, which often overlap and cause more work for all concerned. A great way of supporting colleagues is to support wellbeing by reducing unnecessary workload; all that is needed really is the graduated response (IEPs), annotated planning, use of EP reports or EHCPs as highlighted working documents (by all staff involved with the child), a provision map of interventions (class or whole-school works), and some data tracking or feedback – that is it!

Providing support with individual cases

It would be useful here to look at some worked examples of the possible support SENCOs can provide for colleagues when children in their classes are experiencing difficulties in the four areas of need.

Cognition and learning

Child A in Year 4 has a specific learning difficulty (SpLD), which school suspect could be linked to dyslexia. Orally, he is confident and enjoys discussing his learning. However:

- He reverses bs and ds.
- He has poor phonological awareness and spelling.
- He struggles with writing and puts letters in words in the wrong order.
- He has poor handwriting.
- When reading, he says that the words 'move'.
- He reads very slowly.
- He cannot follow directions and does not know right from left.

His teacher has put strategies in place to help:

- He has visual reminders to help with reversals.
- He is not expected to copy from the board; he has information on a whiteboard on the desk.
- He has a spell checker.

- He has been tried with different-coloured overlays (he says yellow helps with reading) and coloured paper.
- He has extra time to complete written tasks and written homework is kept to a minimum.
- For longer pieces of writing he has a scribe so that he can get his thoughts down on paper quickly.
- He has the opportunity to use a laptop at certain times for writing.

In this case, the SENCO could:

- Try using cloze procedure (where writing is scaffolded so that the child only needs to insert key words into sentences) for some writing tasks to minimise the amount of writing needed.
- Use repetition and overlearning. (Schools who use the whole-school Read Write Inc can access a phonics intervention for Key Stage 2 pupils.)
- Assess for dyslexia. In discussion with parents, it transpires that other members of Child A's family are dyslexic. The SENCO could also try a Nessy screener test. In this case, it reveals that there is a high probability of dyslexia and Child A is put on Nessy Reading and Spelling, which is an independently accessed, multi-sensory computer program. (See Chapter 7, page 85, for more details and to find more information on www.nessy.com, where subscribers can also access specific dyslexia training as well as a range of supportive programs.)

Top tip

It is important that a dyslexic child has access to age-appropriate texts through, for example, the class novel. I can remember an excluded Year 6 child from my primary PRU who could only access very basic Key Stage 1 texts to read but thrived through the class novel, which he was able to discuss in depth and really enjoy. His mother bought him a whole series of books for Christmas and said it was the first time he showed any interest at all in reading. See the British Dyslexia Society (www.bdadyslexia.org.uk) and www.dyslexiaida.org for further help and advice for supporting children with dyslexia.

Communication and interaction

Child B is in the reception class and is struggling to communicate appropriately with adults and peers. He is happy and settled in the class, and no concerns have been passed on by his nursery; however:

- He has difficulty with receptive language; he needs reminders for listening, particularly in a whole-class situation, and misunderstands questions and instructions.
- He can understand concrete language, for example in one-to-one play activities, but struggles with abstract language, such as: 'What did you have for tea last night?'
- He struggles with expressive language and struggles to convey meaning unless as part of a one-to-one play activity with concrete apparatus or toys.
- He has difficulties starting or responding to a conversation, often volunteering information that makes no sense.

His teacher has put strategies in place to help:

- She provides one-to-one support in modelling and discussion during play activities.
- She has asked the in-house SALT to observe and suggest further strategies; she has also expressed concerns and wonders whether he needs to be seen by an educational psychologist.

In this case, the SENCO could:

- Speak with Child B's carer. This reveals the child has suspected glue ear. She has agreed to follow up and we now have a medical appointment; she has reported similar problems in the home.
- Refer the child to NHS SALT provision for a formal investigation of his difficulties; the SENCO may benefit from

an informal discussion with the service first to see whether the referral criteria are met.

- Engage in one-to-one play with the child to assess his difficulties. In play with concrete apparatus, the child was able to communicate appropriately but again struggled with more abstract questioning; interestingly, he could remember the words of a number of nursery rhymes and songs off by heart.
- Recommend that modelling and one-to-one support be continued and that the child should not be expected to answer abstract questions, particularly in a large group situation.

Top tip

For more information contact The Communication Trust website at www.thecommunicationtrust.org.uk. They have a wealth of advice and resources.

SEMH

Child C in Year 1 has social, communication and behavioural problems and can be challenging at times. He will impulsively hit out at others and be defiant to staff; he struggles to follow rules and boundaries. In addition:

- He is impulsive and struggles to behave appropriately.
- He lacks concentration and finds it hard to focus on the task in hand.
- He reacts to others being 'in his space' and will lash out indiscriminately.
- He constantly fidgets and finds sitting still and listening hard.
- He finds it hard at playtimes and other unstructured times.
- He calls out and finds turn-taking hard.
- He finds it hard to make friends and often chooses to play alone.

His teacher has put in place the following strategies:

- Support at playtimes and other unstructured times where possible.
- Reasonable adjustments for him fidgeting on the carpet; consequences are only in place if he hurts another child deliberately.
- The learning mentor is supporting him with friendships.

In this case, the SENCO could:

- Ensure the child has a workstation personalised with his name, a timer, 'now and next' cards and a box of activities to use independently.
- Provide the child with a fiddle toy, which he is taught how to use properly, i.e. it is to help with listening and concentrating and should not be a distraction to self or others.
- Advise that activities are chunked for a few minutes (now) with independent activities, such as a jigsaw (next), and measured by a sand timer.
- In discussion with the parent, who is struggling at home, refer the child to the community paediatrician to look at possible ADHD.
- Open a CAF/TAF and involve the school nurse.
- Refer the family to 'Early Help and Wellbeing' for support at home; the practitioner from this service takes on the role of lead professional and suggests a number of helpful interventions.

Top tip

For more information, contact the ADHD Foundation (www.adhdfoundation.org.uk) or adders.org.

Sensory and physical needs

Child D in Year 6 has very significant hearing loss and has been fitted with hearing aids in both ears; previously she has been fitted with grommets and has been under SALT and the hearing clinic since nursery. I am going to reverse the procedure here as it is for the SENCO to facilitate specialist teacher support, advice and training, which the class teacher will then implement; if as SENCO you are not sure what to do, consult with your LA SEND department, your LA educational psychologist or an experienced colleague in another school – your headteacher should be able to sort this out for you.

In this case, the SENCO could:

- Provide the teacher with relevant specialist support from a deafness professional with regard to training in the use of hearing aids (such as correct fitting) and appropriate classroom strategies.
- Provide regular 'Teacher of the Deaf' support sessions for the teacher; these are accessed through your LA and are usually a bought-in service.
- Ensure that robust transition arrangements are in place from primary to secondary school.
- Liaise with the SEND office to see whether an application for an EHCP can be made so that the child is well supported in her next school.

The child's teacher should put in place the following strategies, with guidance from the SENCO:

- Ensure the child is seated correctly and can see the teacher's face clearly; the teacher or other adult should speak to her directly (and the adult should repeat if she does not hear what is being said).
- Provide access to small-group work or one-to-one sessions to introduce and reinforce concepts.
- Provide visual cues where necessary.
- Give the child extra time for processing information.

Top tip

For further information, advice and support, see the National Deaf Children's Society website (www.ndcs.org.uk). They have a wealth of downloadable resources for children, schools and families.

The important thing to remember is that colleagues will have varying degrees of skill and knowledge in supporting their children with SEND and you, as SENCO, are their first port of call in meeting additional needs outside of quality-first teaching. This does not mean you can know everything, but there is help out there if you need it. To be effective, there needs to be a whole-school, inclusive approach for SEND and consistency of systems across the board. Teachers should feel supported, not criticised. Remember, they are expected to meet the full range of needs in their classes and have heavy workloads (and this applies to you if you have a class teaching responsibility!). It is easy to 'teacher blame' if things are not going well for a child, but being proactive as SENCO with modelling and practical help will give colleagues confidence that they are not 'on their own' and will show that you know what you are doing in your role and can 'walk the walk'.

Chapter takeaways

- Audit one area of provision in your school and check that supportive strategies are in place for those pupils.
- Look at the four areas of need and review your SEND pupils. Is there a consistent approach and are suggested strategies in place?

Chapter 6
Supporting parents

Section 2 of the SEND Code of Practice (Department for Education, 2014a) states plainly what advice and support is available to parents, so it is useful to read through and check that your practice in school reflects statutory requirements. The Local Offer (see Chapter 3) on your council website sets out support for parents; again, it is useful to familiarise yourself with it.

In August 2014, the Department for Education (2014c) published a SEND guide for parents and carers. Written directly for parents and carers, it covers:

- 'What do SEN and disability mean?
- The principles of the system that supports children and young people with SEN or disabilities
- What the law is and what your rights are
- How the system should work
- What early years settings, schools, colleges and other educational providers must do, or should do, to support you and your child
- What your local authority and other services (such as health and social services) must do, or should do, to support you and your child
- What you can do if you disagree with, or want to challenge, decisions that are made by organisations providing support for your child' (p. 5).

The guide also signposts parents to a number of organisations, but information provided via the Local Offer is obviously going to be more useful in terms of services accessible in the local area.

So how can you, as SENCO, support this process in school?

Informing parents when a child is placed on the SEN register

First of all, if any child is assessed at SEN support according to the Code of Practice, and subsequently placed on the SEN register, then parents or carers *must* be informed as soon as possible. It is your job, as SENCO, to have that discussion, although the class teacher may have already raised some concerns with the family. I find this is best done 'informally' rather than in an official-sounding 'meeting', unless there is a CAF or TAF in place or there is involvement from social services. Sometimes, a parent may approach you first with their own concerns, but if not this will need to be handled sensitively, particularly if a parent has not noticed any causes for concern. However, it is better to be honest and open at an early stage, rather than letting problems escalate.

Case study 11

I can always remember, early on as a SENCO, having to have a discussion with a reception child's parent about his social and communication difficulties; he was later diagnosed with ASC-Asperger's and received full-time support from a teaching assistant via a statement (prior to EHCPs) right up until he moved to secondary school. This would not happen, or at least would be very rare, now in mainstream primary! I can still see mum's bewilderment and her saying that she just thought 'he was my little odd-ball!', but he did get the help he needed and his teaching assistant encouraged independence as much as she could, which stood him in good stead when he transitioned to his next school, where he did well.

You also need to be clear in the discussion what the child's difficulties are and how you, as a school, are going to support them (this is an essential part of the 'assess, plan, do, review' cycle; see page 19).

Developing ongoing positive relationships

Parents, as previously stated in Chapter 3, page 31, will have access to your school's SEN information report and policy via the website but, as SENCO, you are the go-to person who makes the process 'real' for families. As an outstanding practitioner, you will be developing positive relationships with your parents, and this can be achieved by good communication and transparency in all areas:

- Parents will want to know what is already being done in class to support their child. It is also important at this stage to emphasise the child's strengths; no parent wants their child to be reframed as a 'problem' – we need to celebrate the great things about them!
- If you feel the child has unmet needs, have a proper dialogue about this. It often transpires that parents have also noticed things at home, but regardless parents do not want to be 'talked at'; they need to be part of a discussion.
- Once you have had this initial dialogue, you can then suggest actions that might now be undertaken, for example asking the family doctor to refer on to community paediatrics; in some cases, schools can refer directly.
- It is important to talk to staff, observe and work with the child, and talk to them before seeing the parents; pupil voice is a very important part of the statutory framework and this can be done through discussion or even simple drawings.
- Through observation and discussion, you can get a clear picture of where the child needs extra support, over and above quality-first teaching; if anything needs changing or tweaking it can be put in place straight away.

What makes a good SENCO: the parental view

I thought I would #asktwitter (I interact with a range of parents and professionals there) what makes a good SENCO from a parental point of view and got the following responses.

Good SENCOs:

- understand and respect the law and the rights of individuals
- are approachable, supportive and accessible
- value parental knowledge and skills
- are non-judgemental and inclusive of parents and pupils
- know their knowledge and skills limitations and are honest about them
- will seek professional advice and guidance
- are honest about the limitations of school and LEA systems
- honestly discuss academic potential and progression
- speak about the child as a person rather than a thing or problem to fix – relationships are important
- are open – there is a willingness to risk saying 'I don't know' if uncertain and to invite ideas and feedback (both build trust)
- give feedback about interventions and outcomes, and listen to intervention suggestions from parents
- know that their approach in SEND is more important than their knowledge (parents don't expect you to know everything, but to want to learn)
- work together to solve problems
- have a willingness to explore opportunities, not just listening to the parent or child but actively putting into practice their ideas
- listen, care, assume competence and are not dishonest
- understand that some communicate differently
- understand the power imbalance and are never patronising
- remove barriers, are inclusive and offer partnership not tokenism
- appreciate that each and every child is different (there is no such thing as 'typical' for any diagnosis and assuming there is is just laziness on the professional's part)
- are part of a team that collaborates, follows through and most importantly believes our child belongs… it changes everything.

The fabulous thing about being a SENCO is the ability to be integral to practice that changes everything. The core of the above thread is about listening, trust, belief, collaboration, caring and above all the ability to form positive relationships with children and families. Outstanding practice has this at its very heart.

How to speak with parents

I also asked Twitter which phrases parents disliked most or found most unhelpful when talking to SENCOs. They said:

- 'They're fine in school. It must be a home problem.' (This led to school refusal – the child refused to go back into school.)
- 'He doesn't seem that autistic.'
- 'He's fine in school.' (No, he's just masking and will explode as soon as we get in the car.)
- Opinions on behaviour with no training or evidence.
- 'Trust us' used in isolation. (This sounds a lot like silencing.)
- 'He' (child) is not that bad… We have had much worse.' (This was said about one parent's autistic son transitioning to secondary school.)
- 'The SENCO doesn't have a clue and we are on our own. He struggles socially, hides in the library every lunchtime and no one cares! Outstanding school!' (This was said by a parent.)
- 'We feel…' instead of 'How do you feel about…'.
- 'Trust us, we know what we're doing' (without the follow-through to show they actually do).
- 'She just wants to be like everyone else' (as an excuse not to differentiate).
- 'She won't get an EHCP.'
- 'Oh yes, they all find Year 7 exhausting, don't they?'
- Referring to parent as 'mum' in meetings with other professionals.
- 'Child A isn't "accessing the curriculum"' (which means the school hasn't adapted it to capture the child's interest and meet their needs!).

- 'He needs to be independent.'
- 'He is doing it on purpose.'
- 'When she chooses to, she... However...' (implying that her autism is a choice).
- 'We'll wait and see.'
- 'This is about her behaviour, not her needs, and that's not our responsibility' (referring to putting things in place that would meet her needs).

Now it may be on occasion you know you are guilty of saying one or more of the above (I know I am) but outstanding practice comes from realising and learning from your mistakes. It comes from treating others with respect and giving them a voice. There is a perception in some quarters that parents (particularly of SEND children) can be 'difficult' and 'make a fuss' or 'want a label'; others can be seen as 'neglectful' or 'uncaring' or have 'poor parenting skills'. What you need to remember is that just as all children have different needs, so do their parents; when I was at the PRU I saw how disengaged parents of excluded children were with the whole school process and it often brought back to them difficulties that they experienced at school themselves. Most of all, they wanted help – help for their children and for themselves – in a non-judgemental way, without finger pointing.

The world for parents of children with SEND can be a scary place as there are so many seemingly insurmountable obstacles to overcome. Many parents have to fight for the rights of their children, particularly when statutory assessment is needed (this will be discussed in more detail in Chapter 9, page 115), and need support and reassurance. Poor practice arises from:

- A child's difficulties not being correctly identified and supported.
- Quality-first teaching not meeting the child's needs, for example a lack of differentiation, where the SENCO does not recognise this and parents are consequently unaware.
- Poor recognition of a variety of needs, such as ASD, ADHD and SLCN, and misconceptions surrounding possible diagnosis. See the comment above: 'He doesn't seem that autistic...'

- Poor or non-existent relationships with the child and subsequently the parent (which is why observation and working with the child are so important).
- Lack of organisation in school and agreed procedures not being followed, for example concerns from class teachers not being followed up and referrals to relevant professionals, such as SALT, not being made; this can lead to negative perceptions of the school by parents, quite understandably.
- Excuses being made for lack of action, which compounds the problem.
- Not speaking to parents straight away when a difficulty is identified.
- Assuming knowledge that is not backed up by experience or training; parents know when they are being fobbed off!
- Failure to follow the graduated approach – assess, plan, do, review. This may well lead to the assumption that 'She won't get an EHCP.'
- A change of SENCO: this can be very frustrating for parents, particularly if they have a positive relationship with the outgoing SENCO. Trust needs to be built up as soon as possible.
- Lack of time to do the job properly; many SENCOs have class teaching responsibilities and only a limited time to do the job. If this is the case, be honest with the parent and speak to senior leaders about having more time, even if it is for a 'one-off' action or meeting.
- A poor attitude, not seeing a parent's viewpoint, losing patience, being patronising and negative body language; one Twitter comment mentioned 'sighing, hunching shoulders and eye rolls'. Sometimes, attitudes from senior leaders can 'rub off' on the SENCO; they may pass on their own negativity by using words such as 'pushy parent', 'attention seeker' or 'over-protective'.

Top tip

Before you talk to parents, jot down the main points you want to discuss in the meeting and avoid being drawn into arguments or confrontation – there can be emotional scenes prompted by the parent not being convinced enough is being done, or not wanting to hear the problem, but it is your job to stay calm and diffuse anxiety and show that you genuinely care. Always work with the parent and don't take up 'positions' even if you think you are right; remember the child's needs should stay at the forefront of discussion.

Signposting parents to further support

It may be that you will need to signpost parents to further support in helping them navigate SEND systems; again, the Local Offer on the county website should list all the organisations that a parent can access to provide that support. These will include:

- The Information, Advice and Support (IAS) Team: They provide information on regulations and guidance, health and social care, and support from other agencies. They can support families with regard to liaising between parents, schools and other professionals, school exclusion and managing appeals. I always signpost parents to this as they are often unaware of what is on the Local Offer; I also show parents the website and how to navigate it so that they can read relevant information for themselves.
- Advocacy services: These services support parental voice. The website www.advocacyfocus.org.uk gives advice on getting help.
- Independent Parental Special Education Advice (IPSEA): A charity that offers legal advice, support and training to ensure children access the right education support and can provide representation at tribunals.
- Special Needs Jungle: Their website, www.specialneedsjungle.com, provides information, news and resources for parents of children with SEND.
- Specialist organisations: Organisations such as the National Autistic Society (NAS) offer help and advice for parents.

- Parent support groups in the local area: It is useful to keep a list of local support groups so that you can signpost parents to them; look out for free early intervention services (this may be linked to the opening of a CAF), as they can provide support holistically for all the family and work in the home.

Facilitating meetings between parents and external agencies

As SENCO, it is important to make sure that you facilitate meetings between parents and LEA SEND departments. Specifically, this involves:

- Meetings with educational psychologists: When it is decided that the child would benefit from the involvement of an educational psychologist, parents should always be invited to speak to the SENCO and educational psychologist after an observation or assessment has been undertaken.
- Annual reviews: These are when there are significant changes to be made to the EHCP or a change in provision, such as a potential move to specialist provision or requests for increased funding (SENDO and EP to attend); in an annual review with no significant changes to the plan, the LA do not usually attend, although this may vary from county to county, so please ask.
- TAF meetings: These are when discussing an application for statutory assessment (EHCPs) (SENDO and EP to attend); otherwise TAF meetings will be held at regular intervals with parents and other relevant agencies not in SEND departments.
- Co-production meetings: These occur preferably when the EHCP is in draft form, although changes can be made after the final plan has been issued if parents have not been given that opportunity; often this can happen when drafts are issued over holiday periods and have to be finalised within a certain timescale (SENDO to attend).
- Transition meetings: These occur where a child with an EHCP will experience a significant change, for example a move from

nursery to primary school, a move from primary school to secondary school, or a move to special school (EP to attend).

Case study 12

A child at the PRU obtained an EHCP for specialist provision and a draft plan was issued. The SENDO arranged a co-production meeting with the school and parents to discuss the plan and go through it line by line. This gave parents and the school (specifically the SENCO) the opportunity to ensure that the plan was fit for purpose, accurate and tailored to meet the child's needs; the parents were confident that they were fully involved in the process and knew the goals that the school would be working towards with the child. The school was also clear about next steps in ensuring that the plan was supporting the pupil appropriately.

Case study 13

It is also useful, where possible, for parents to meet with other professionals coming into, or working within, the setting with their child; one school I am in currently (which has a social worker and SALT) has drop-in sessions for parents on a weekly basis. I also ensure that the specialist teacher attends meetings or at least provides a report; it is important that parents have a clear picture of what is being done to support their child. I also meet or exchange phone calls with parents regularly so that they know what is happening, for example the outcomes of referrals or how the child is managing. If there is funding available, I do try to enlist support from specialist services, such as for autism, which may be to get further advice or access training.

Chapter takeaways

- Check that you are up to date in knowing available services for parents and being able to point them in a helpful direction.
- Evaluate the needs of your SEND children with regard to how you involve parents in decision-making and collaborative working.

Chapter 7
Useful interventions and resources

In this chapter I want to look at a range of interventions and resources that are available to support children with SEND; obviously some are commercial and come at a price, but many are free and effective. As SENCO it can be difficult to decide which interventions or resources are worth investing in and which are not, but hopefully this chapter will provide a starting point or at least open up discussions and reflections about which interventions or resources are useful. For ease, I will organise them according to the four areas of need. As you read through this chapter, please note that this list is not exhaustive as there is so much out there!

Communication and interaction

Nasen (www.nasen.org.uk) is a subscription site (for schools and individuals) that provides a wealth of resources that are effective at 'both a practical day-to-day and strategic level'. These include:

- 'Useful, time-saving templates
- Guidance and information
- Top tips
- Articles
- Evidence-based ideas for practice
- Nasen Journals' (Nasen, 2015).

Nasen are influential and well respected at national level; they are a provider partner for the NASENCo award and it is worth considering a subscription for your school. They have a number of resources to support SLCN, including a webinar (June 2018) on practical suggestions to enhance classroom practice.

The Communication Trust website (www.thecommunicationtrust.org.uk) is a 'coalition of over 50 not-for-profit organisations' supporting SLCN in schools. The Trust offers numerous CPD opportunities and practitioner resources. They have launched a free CPD short online course called 'An introduction to speech, language and communication', which is tailored for practitioners from Early Years up to further education; see www.thecommunicationtrust.org.uk/projects/professional-development/online-short-course.

Twinkl (www.twinkl.com) is a subscription website chock-full of useful resources and they have a whole section on SLCN, including games, activities, PowerPoint prompts and training – for example, there is a useful 'Teaching Assistant Resource Pack' and visual timetables.

Talking tins are a great resource for promoting the development of speaking and listening. You can use them to record and play back speech. These are widely available from educational outlets.

There are a number of interventions popular in schools including:

- Wellcomm speech and language toolkit: Suitable for six months to six years (see www.gl-assessment.co.uk), this is an easy-to-administer screening tool and has a wealth of supportive resources.
- Time to Talk (Ginger the Bear): A commercial intervention that helps to teach and develop spoken language and social interaction skills to children aged four to eight years, with the help of the teddy Ginger the Bear; for more information see the LDA website (www.ldalearning.com). There is also a Time to Talk board game.
- Talk Boost: A commercial targeted intervention for children aged four to seven years with language delay. See www.talkingpoint.org.uk.

Ask around in your school cluster or SENCO group which interventions they use in school and which work well, and be cautious – whatever you choose needs to meet the needs of your school; it may be a case of trial and error but try to avoid expensive resources that may or may not be cost-effective. If possible, ask for a free trial or have a look in another school.

Cognition and learning

This area of need can cover a whole spectrum of learning difficulties and have associated issues with working memory, retention and poor expressive and processing difficulties. I find it is necessary to consult with specialists, such as paediatricians, SALT and educational psychologists, to try to unpick these as they can be complex and have an underlying medical cause; also there is often an overlap between the four areas of need, for example ADHD can cross over into SEMH (which is where I will address this). Specific learning difficulties include dyslexia and dyscalculia.

Dyslexia

Dyslexia affects the way a child processes, stores and retrieves information, with memory and processing problems, storage and retrieval issues, and poor sequencing and organisation. It can affect words and numbers and may mean that a child reverses letters (often b and d) or mixes letters up in a word; the child may have difficulties with reading and spelling and find writing a struggle. See the British Dyslexia Association website (www.bdadyslexia.org.uk) for more information.

There are a number of interventions and resources to support dyslexia, including the following:

- Educational software (commercial), such as Word Shark and Number Shark (see www.wordshark.co.uk for more details of both). I have found these to be very powerful as they are presented in the form of games, which is very motivating for the children; Nessy Dyslexia Quest (a commercial screening tool) measures possible factors for dyslexia and Nessy Reading and Spelling (also suitable for children with EAL) is a structured programme to support pupils with dyslexia or dyslexic tendencies. Again these are both presented in a cartoon-game format. IDL Literacy (see www.idlcloud.co.uk) is a popular intervention to help improve reading and spelling for those children with dyslexia or dyslexic tendencies.

- The Stile Tray for dyslexia (see www.ldalearning.com) is a specially structured self-checking programme.
- Twinkl (www.twinkl.co.uk) have a number of (commercial) resources to assist pupils with dyslexia.
- There are other resources such as coloured overlays, often linked to Meares-Irlen Syndrome (see www.irlen.com for more information), and the use of different-coloured paper to write on or different-coloured computer typefaces, tinted glasses, the use of alphabet arrays using magnetic letters to help with ordering and spelling, laptops or touch-typing programs to help with writing composition, scribing to assist extended writing, and speech-to-writing or writing organisation programs such as Clicker 7 (see www.cricksoft.com for more information).

Again, speak to fellow professionals; the technology side of education is proceeding at a rapid rate so there may be other programs out there that are equally effective.

Dyscalculia

Dyscalculia is a mathematics learning disorder; children struggle with counting, basic maths, fractions, graphs, money and time yet are often not struggling in other subjects. See www.dyscalculia.org and the British Dyslexia Association website (www.bdadyslexia.org.uk) for more information.

Teachwire (www.teachwire.net) have six games for pupils with dyscalculia that look really good as they are multi-sensory. Mathletics (see uk.mathletics.com) is a computer program that supports all learning styles in maths and can be accessed independently at the pupil's own level; it is very visual and interactive and supports pupils at every stage of their mathematical development.

The use of practical apparatus and simple overlearning activities such as precision teaching may help in this area.

Working memory difficulties

Cogmed (www.cogmed.com.au) have a great 'Working Memory Checklist' from pre-school onwards but there is a wealth of resources out there. Ask around to see what works in your local schools. Be careful of working memory ICT programs (there are a range of these available to buy, although they are often expensive); there is a theory that using these improves the ability to access that program rather than improving memory! However, there are simple, free resources that exercise the brain, for example card games such as 'Pairs' where children have to memorise the whereabouts of a particular card to form a 'pair'; this does not have to use the whole deck – I often start with just the picture cards and then build up. The 'tray game' is also another good example: showing the child a range of objects on a tray and then removing it, asking the child to see how many items they can remember; again the number of objects can be built up. The great thing with these simple games is that they can be reinforced and practised at home, and parental interaction and support are the key to these being successful!

A home–school diary can be very useful and also a notebook where the child or the teacher can jot notes to form an aide-memoire for remembering key concepts.

Pre-teaching is a strategy in which teachers introduce new concepts or specialist vocabulary (for science, for example) to a child prior to the lesson or series of lessons. The idea is that a seed is planted that will help the child grasp the new ideas when they encounter them again in the lesson. This is particularly useful for children who have poor working memory issues.

Scaffolding, task ladders and chunking are also useful strategies. The child is given a 'starter' sheet with some initial text relating to the activity already entered; many children with memory or inattention difficulties 'freeze' when presented with a blank piece of paper! They respond well to activities being 'chunked' in accessible small 'bites' so that activities can be completed bit by bit, which does not put a strain on recall. A task ladder is a guide that provides short instructions on how to complete a task in a simple form; this could be laminated and kept on the child's desk.

Precision teaching is a programme that promotes overlearning of basic concepts that are often lost from working memory; for more information and free resources to support the programme, see John Taylor's 'Freebies' at www.johnandgwyn.co.uk. I can thoroughly recommend this intervention. Your educational psychologist may be able to provide specific training (mine did). It only takes a few minutes each day and can be delivered by either a teacher or a trained member of your support staff; I was able to cascade training through school, which is great as it is impossible to personally have a hand on everything!

Case study 14

A Year 4 pupil is really struggling to remember key concepts and is responding well to overlearning techniques. Phonics is an area she struggles with despite having a lot of one-to-one and small-group input in addition to quality-first teaching. It was agreed with the class teacher that she would have precision teaching for key words linked to Phase 2 phonics and after a slow start she was able to speedily develop recall of them. We then changed it to giving her the meaning so she could find the word, as this was the next area she struggled with; again she demonstrated good progress over time. We are now concentrating on her showing this in related areas such as writing sentences and spelling activities.

There are a number of commercial programmes that employ overlearning as a way of grasping phonics, but these are whole-school initiatives and need careful investigation before adoption. Their prescriptiveness can throw up a range of difficulties further down the line in relation to independent writing (although they can be very effective for a child who struggles with basic sounds).

Social, emotional and mental health (SEMH)

Autism

There is a wealth of resources for children with SEMH related to autism and links can be found on the following websites:

- For autism, see www.autism.org.uk (National Autistic Society) and www.reachoutasc.com (Reachout ASC, Lynn McCann). Lynn McCann (2018) also has a practical book of social stories called *Stories That Explain*, which gives a range of social stories covering every area of difficulty.
- Twinkl (www.twinkl.com) have practical resources for children who are on the spectrum, for example visual timetables.

There are many recommended strategies for children on the spectrum but it is important that each child is treated as an individual as no two children are alike. Some suggested generic strategies are:

- Aids to help with sensory needs: For example ear defenders for those children who are noise sensitive, fiddle toys for those who need calming strategies and chewables for children with pica.
- Visual timetables: Children with ASC often need changes to be flagged up in advance, with adjustments to the daily timetable communicated straight away to the child. The visual timetable gives order and structure to the day and can be linked to activities so that the child can 'post' completed tasks before moving on to the next.
- 'Now and next' cards: Agree a time to complete an activity (five or ten minutes) – this can be supported by the use of an egg timer – and then offer a choice of activities (chosen by the child with scaffolding from the adult). This feeds the child's need to 'be in charge' within adult rules or boundaries.
- Social stories: These explain simple scenarios that autistic children struggle with and give help and reinforcement of appropriate self-regulation strategies.
- Individual workstations: Some children with ASC respond well to having an individual space to aid concentration and prevent distraction from others. There are a range of 'pop-up' screens that can be put on a child's desk, all the way up to workstations that have space for visual timetables, 'now and next' cards and other appropriate resources.

Case study 15

J is a pupil in reception who is presenting with significant social, emotional and communication difficulties. He has not had an assessment by professionals but would benefit from a paediatric referral to look at possible underlying medical needs. J struggles to interact positively with his peers and is happy to play alone. He dislikes other children encroaching on his personal space and will have 'meltdowns' with very few apparent triggers. He takes a long time to settle down and will become emotional and cry big tears. He is hyposensitive to touch and craves firm hugs to calm him.

J does require a high amount of adult one-to-one attention to keep him on track or he will become disruptive. In class J struggles to sit in his carpet space and has the opportunity to sit in a chair at the back of the group; however, he becomes upset if other children then sit in his carpet space. J has obsessions and is currently obsessed by cats, following work on the book *Six Dinner Sid*. He enjoys dressing up in a cat costume and behaving like a cat.

J struggles to interact as part of a whole class and presents as not understanding basic instructions or requests. J has been tested by his class teacher, who is also the school SENCO, and his profile is very uneven and spiky; his scores are particularly low on emotions and empathy and he seems to have little understanding of even basic requests and one-step instructions.

J's teachers say he easily loses interest in his lessons, particularly when more abstract concepts are being discussed, and without one-to-one support he becomes very disruptive. I observed him in PE and he could copy other children to a point but then ran about doing his own thing; he could not follow adult instructions unless these were explicitly modelled for him. He needs to be constantly watched and will act inappropriately if adult attention is not focused on him. J is operating well below age-related expectations and needs a personalised curriculum with short activities that are a mixture of adult-supported and independent tasks he can access at his own level.

J presents as a child whose behaviours are indicative of possible ASD or ADHD and these are a barrier to his learning. He is restless, fidgety and impulsive and struggles with social communication; he appears, at times, to be unable to control his impulsiveness and can have meltdowns, which puts others at risk. J has significant developmental delay both in speech and behaviour and would benefit from some medical assessments.

The agreed actions in this case were:

1. J would benefit from a referral to a paediatrician to look at possible ASD and this needs to be facilitated as soon as possible; supporting evidence needs to be supplied by school. An individual behaviour plan and risk assessment will be initiated (and shared with all staff) if behaviours continue to escalate.
2. The school needs to have a bank of strategies to help J access the class more positively, particularly at times when he is struggling with the curriculum. These could include:
   a. a visual timetable so he knows what to expect in the day
   b. a box of activities close at hand so that he can access 'now... then', i.e. a short, focused activity a few minutes long followed by a chosen activity of his own (a timer would be beneficial)
   c. an individual work space in class, personalised with his name, visual timetable, chosen activities, a cuddly toy (possibly from home), a blanket to calm him by meeting his sensory needs, and a mirror to reinforce his sense of self and emotions work (this space can be used as a calming-down area)
   d. tapping into his interests, for example cats, to engage him in discussion
   e. adult modelling of appropriate behaviours and actions and engaging alongside him to help and encourage
   f. work on basic emotions, such as happy and sad.
3. J responds well to familiar routines and is showing some independence; encourage him by careful structuring of his day via a visual timetable.
4. J needs practice in following one-step instructions, with adults maintaining appropriate eye contact and saying his name first.
5. Triggers should be noted via ABC sheets (ABC refers to Antecedents, Behaviours, Consequences or, put simply, what led up to a behaviour, what the behaviour looked like and what the consequences of the behaviour were) or similar; pre-emptive strategies, such as distraction, should be used where possible.
6. Advice from an educational psychologist would be useful at some point and a detailed graduated response should be maintained as an evidence base for future action if needed.

The above strategies were put in place with positive results and evidence is being collated, in line with the graduated response, for an EHCP.

ADHD

See the ADHD Foundation website at www.adhdfoundation.org.uk and online information for ADD and ADHD at www.adders.org.uk. Many of the strategies for children with ASD mirror those for children with ADD and ADHD. These include:

- Individual workstations: Children with ADHD are easily distracted by what is going on around them and often distract others from their learning. The workstations (which can be simple desk screens) help with this as they keep the child focused on their learning.
- Visual timetables: These can reduce anxiety by signposting what is coming next. Children with ADHD tend to be disorganised and stressed about changes to which they have not been signposted.
- Now and next: These are short, focused activities that can often be scaffolded by the use of an egg timer with a follow-up from a box of (chosen) activities to enhance an individual independent activity.
- Social stories: These can work if focused on the desired outcome through reinforcement of appropriate strategies.

Boxall

Boxall is an appropriate intervention to use with children with identified SEMH, including attachment issues. So what is Boxall?

The Boxall Profile provides a framework for the precise assessment of children who have social, emotional and behavioural difficulties (SEMH) and are failing at school. It helps teachers to plan interventions for children whose behaviour seems to make no sense. The profile provides the teacher with insights and suggests points of entry into the child's world – it makes people think what lies behind the behaviour. For more information see: www.nurtureuk.org/introducing-nurture/boxall-profile.

Boxall is a vital tool for children with SEMH, especially those receiving nurture provision; it identifies the gaps in a child's SEMH and provides interventions to address these.

Case study 16

The below analysis is based on a series of questions and an examination of the answers according to the Boxall Profile (see website www.nurtureuk.org/introducing-nurture/boxall-profile for more information; please note it is a paid-for resource).

Boxall is a tool that comes in a paper copy or website (subscription required) and comprises two sections: Section one – Developmental Strands, which looks at aspects of the child's development, and Section two – The Diagnostic Profile, which examines social and emotional development with a focus on attachment. In each section, there are a series of questions relating to areas of development delineated and grouped by a specific heading, e.g. Inconsequential behaviour, and a letter of the alphabet. These headings are then scored individually. The profile gives clear instructions on how to do this.

Beyond the Boxall is a resource that analyses the questions grouped for each area, e.g. Purposeful attention is defined by questions 1, 6, 12 and 20 and gives appropriate strategies to try to 'close the gaps' in those learning or SEMH areas.

Analysis of Boxall Profile for J

The two main areas of focus are 'Section A: Purposeful attention' in 'Developmental Strands' and 'Section T: Inconsequential behaviour' under 'Diagnostic Profile'. Interestingly, given the nature of his child looked after (CLA) background, J apparently scores 'within the norm' for attachment difficulties; however, the very clear message from Section T is that his inconsequential behaviours are attachment-driven according to 'Beyond the Boxall' analysis.

Section A: Purposeful attention

J's low scores show that J is developmentally immature. He is inattentive, lacks concentration and is unable to follow simple requests or instructions. He may have difficulty understanding the expectations of the school and in predicting adult responses to his behaviour.

Areas of difficulty Qs 1, 6, 12 and 20.

Strategies to help (in class and one to one) as recommended by Beyond the Boxall:

- Use J's name before giving him an instruction and encourage eye contact.

- Consider whether J can understand the concepts being taught or discussed.
- Consider whether he has been sitting for too long.
- Teach and model specific skills.
- Provide routine, structure and consistency.
- Provide short, achievable tasks followed by an element of self-chosen activity; for example at the end of his maths work he asked for one last game of 'Times Table Bingo' and this kept him calm and focused.
- Give rewards and stickers – he enjoyed getting a green dojo for spelling.
- Find him a buddy – his one-to-one support could be this; he benefits from forming positive relationships.
- Use memory and listening games (one to one), for example 'Pairs' using a small number of cards and Kim's Game (memorising a tray of objects and recalling them after they have been covered or removed), and Dobble™ (a commercial game that requires you to pick out matching pictures from a range of objects on two cards – there is only ever one match available) is great for this too!

Section T: Inconsequential behaviour

J is impulse-driven; his personal organisation and identity are underdeveloped. These features suggest that J has had too little help in his early years to gain the resources to relate to others and engage at an age-appropriate level. However, because the behaviours described are normal at an early level, there is an available potential for attachment and growth if appropriate relationships and experiences are provided.

Areas of difficulty Qs 6, 16, 27 and 33.

Strategies to help (in class and one to one) from Beyond the Boxall:

- Adult modelling of appropriate responses.
- Consistent structure and routine with limits, boundaries and clear consequences.
- Calm and consistent responses – do not react. (This works well, as both J's teacher and teaching assistants modelled these successfully.)
- Short, structured activities – select ones that specifically develop concentration linked to J's interests.
- Some work on feelings and emotions – one to one and PSHE.
- Help J recognise and value his own personal abilities, whilst recognising things he needs to improve.

In summary, Boxall is a vital tool in identifying and supporting SEMH and provides good evidence towards the process of assess, plan, do, review.

Mental health

Mental health in children is a massive issue, and there is funding being put into schools to tackle issues and problems. Leading charities Young Minds (youngminds.org.uk) and Mind (www.mind.org.uk) have a wealth of advice, support and resources for children, young people, parents and schools. There are a number of initiatives being rolled out for primary-aged children and their teachers; Heads Together (www.headstogether.org.uk) is launching a free website, 'Mentally Healthy Schools', in conjunction with a number of charity partners including the Royal Foundation (see www.mentallyhealthyschools.org.uk). Content is provided in four areas:

- teaching resources
- risks and protective factors
- mental health needs
- 'whole school approach' for school leaders.

This is a fantastic website! It is easy to navigate and provides links to a host of free and paid-for resources from other providers that have been thoroughly evaluated and 'rated'. It provides information on all aspects of mental health, including anxiety issues (I am coming across these a lot in primary schools) and looks in detail at risks and protective factors and building up resilience. It may be, as SENCO, you will be asked to take on or support a mental health lead in school and the site covers whole-school approaches as well as individual and small-group work. It is stressed that schools are not expected to be substitutes for expert professionals, such as CAMHS or clinical psychologists, but there is plenty that schools can be doing to increase resilience. Emotionally healthy children are more likely to be ready to learn and achieve as they will have high self-esteem and wellbeing.

PSHE

The previous website covers PSHE and circle times with links to reliable resources. The PSHE Association (www.pshe-association.org.uk) has a library of resources including planning toolkits and top tips. A number of websites offer resources, including Twinkl (www.twinkl.com). Owlcation (owlcation.com) have free circle time games and activities with learning objectives.

> **Top tip**
>
> There will be a PSHE co-ordinator in school who may also be asked to take on the lead for mental health; as an outstanding SENCO, it is worth collaborating with that colleague to promote emotional wellbeing as there is an overlap of your roles.

Restorative approaches

Restorative justice has to be part of a whole-school approach, but it is worth looking at the Restorative Justice Council website (restorative-justice.org.uk) for information on restorative approaches for schools. There is a great YouTube video, 'Child's Hill School and Restorative Approaches' (www.youtube.com/watch?v=AJWgayvuWXw), which shows how these can be embedded in a school, with a positive impact on behaviour and wellbeing. This would easily form part of a whole-school approach to mental health and wellbeing.

Sensory and/or physical needs

Children may have sensory and/or physical needs that require specific interventions. For children with physical needs, for example spina bifida, where the spine is under-developed and there is a gap in it, there may be a range of symptoms, including problems with movement, and bladder and bowel problems. The child will have a range of medical specialists scaffolding their care – doctors, paediatricians, occupational therapists and physiotherapists; these specialists will recommend in-house interventions, such as OT, physio (visits from professionals) and OT programmes that schools can deliver.

Interventions for sensory needs may be needed in the form of access to specific equipment such as sensory toys, rooms (if available), strategies for calming and reducing anxiety, e.g. use of chew toys, ear defenders and access to quiet spaces, and modelling of calming-down activities such as slow breathing or counting back.

For hearing or visually impaired children, again it is vital that medical advice is followed and specialist teachers in these fields work with the child (they can be contacted through your local authority specialist teacher service and the school may have to pay for some of the support; in my LEA, initial support hours are provided free of charge).

Chapter takeaways

- Browse through the suggested resources and links in this chapter and prioritise those you need most in the first instance, based on the needs of the pupils in your school.
- Develop a resource plan to match the four areas of need and share relevant information with staff in your school.

Chapter 8
Working with outside agencies

One of the trickiest aspects of being a SENCO is liaising with outside agencies – not because they are not doing their jobs but because services can be unpredictable and subject to changes and cuts. In this chapter I will look at the services you will need to engage with. I will explain the function of these services, provide case studies of how schools work with them in practice, highlight positives and negatives of each service, and offer ways forward to work with them more effectively.

Speech and language therapy (SALT)

Who are they?

Speech and language therapists are employed by the NHS. The website Health Careers (www.healthcareers.nhs.uk) describes the work of a therapist as someone who helps children with:

- 'mild, moderate or severe learning difficulties
- physical difficulties
- language delay
- specific difficulties in producing sounds
- hearing impairment

- cleft lip and palate
- stammering
- autism/social interaction difficulties
- dyslexia
- voice disorders
- selective mutism
- mental health
- developmental language disorder.' (Health Careers, 2015a)

SALT can work directly with schools, and some LEAs have generic application procedures for schools to access with parental permission. Parents can also refer in through their family doctors and schools can support this process with a letter outlining the needs of the child. The Communication Trust (2014) highlights the work of SALT, outlining the following procedures for schools. They say 'Speech and language therapists play an important role in supporting schools to meet the needs of children with SLCN'. Their core purpose is to:

- Support senior leaders to ensure communication-supportive practice throughout their school or setting.
- Provide assessment, including screening or more specific assessment to determine specific areas of need or strategies to support development.
- Provide input for formal assessment, e.g. EHC needs assessment, social and communication panel (ASC assessment).
- Provide training opportunities for school staff, e.g. training in ASD or social stories (this is offered in my area at a low cost, so is affordable).
- Deliver programmes for individual children/small groups – this has worked well in the school I am SENCO in.
- Work closely with families and professionals.
- Support good practice in the classroom through modelling useful resources.

- Support educational target setting and evaluation.
- Work with others to support targeted interventions and support for children.
- Play a vital role in working directly with a child with specific SLCN as well as support the teachers and teaching assistants to differentiate the curriculum appropriately, and provide necessary training.

As well as NHS providers, there are a number of private individuals and companies available for schools to 'buy in' to supplement NHS provision; these can be valuable as they will work with individuals and small groups and provide training for staff.

Case study 17

D has been referred to local SALT provision as he has poor social and communication skills and is potentially autistic. The therapist sees him with mum and then asks to come and observe him in school. She talks to the teacher and suggests work that could be done in school; she also notices that the small group on D's table would benefit from the same strategies and leaves activities that will promote interaction within the group. D's mum discusses her concerns about possible autism and the therapist agrees to refer D to community paediatrics. The paediatrician sees D and collates information from several sources in preparation for referral to the speech and communication panel, which is a collection of medical professionals who will look at the evidence and recommend whether a diagnosis should be given.

Case study 18

F has been referred to the speech and communication panel and has been given a diagnosis of autism. The SALT professional came into school to observe him and offer strategies and training to the teacher and teaching assistant in class. The teaching assistant is accessing a social stories course at a reduced rate and will cascade training to colleagues. A whole-school training session for all staff is also being planned.

Case study 19

Private SALT provider G has conducted a number of assessments for reception-aged children and highlighted a number who need referring to the NHS service for more intensive support. She also takes small groups to improve conversation skills.

Pros and cons

Pros:

- In some areas schools can refer in directly, with parental permission, which means that SALT get a good picture of the child's difficulties.
- Where there is great provision, this can be life-changing for the child with SLCN.
- Private providers, whilst expensive, can ensure a continuity of provision within the school.

Cons:

- There can be a huge turnover of therapists in the NHS, with local SALT professionals moving to other areas; it is important for schools to develop a good relationship with SALT as they provide a vital service as outlined above.
- Waiting times can be lengthy and some children may not get the one-to-one help they need; often SALT programmes are devolved to schools, who are often stretched in providing that support regularly.
- Take-up is dependent on parents making the appointments rather than being offered them; if not, families are discharged immediately. Some parents have not received an offer of an appointment due to postal issues or they mislay them. It is often the most vulnerable children who miss out.

Educational psychologists

Who are they?

Educational psychologists are employed by local education authorities to work in partnership with families, schools and other professionals to help children who are having difficulties with their learning. They:

- Assess children in the school setting, liaising with parents and schools, taking into account the findings of other professionals such as paediatricians, SALT, CAMHS and specialist teachers; the aim is to determine how children can be given the best targeted support in becoming more successful learners.
- May administer cognitive tests as part of the above process.
- Offer appropriate strategies and support as part of the graduated response that schools are required to follow. These could relate to the learning environment, teaching approaches, recommendations for further professional input, advice on the curriculum, behaviour support, practical resources, learning programmes, books for further reading and advice on appropriate staffing.
- Maintain up-to-date research to support best practice, policy and research, to inform recommendations and add to local knowledge.
- Produce written reports summarising the steps needed for a particular child.
- Can provide training for a range of professionals, for example looking at attachment issues and demonstrating precision teaching or Lego™ therapy, and recommend tried-and-tested strategies from other sources.
- Have a duty to support all statutory work such as EHCP annual reviews, changes in provision for pupils with statements and transition arrangements from one setting to another.

Schools apply directly to the local authority for educational psychologist support. There may be a form to complete and parental permission is essential – your local SEND office will advise. Usually, schools are allocated a particular link professional, although this may vary depending on the authority. In some areas, there is currently a shortage of educational psychologists so schools may be grouped into clusters to access advice and support. Many schools buy into private educational psychologist services if they need a child to be assessed urgently, but obviously this can be an expensive option and is dependent on school budgets.

Case study 20

I requested educational psychologist support for F and precision teaching was recommended. The educational psychologist trained our cluster and gave us the relevant materials to deliver it. I was able to cascade this to support staff, with a teacher to oversee the process, and it is now embedded in the school, which is useful for many of our children with poor working memories who benefit from overlearning techniques.

Pros and cons

Pros:

- If the school has access to a familiar link educational psychologist then that person will be familiar with your school context and may be able to direct strategies that support a number of your pupils; also, you can develop a really good reciprocal relationship, so that you can ask for help when needed.
- If your authority has good educational psychologist-to-school ratios, they may be able to support your non-statutory queries and come in to observe pupils.
- Your educational psychologist may be able to offer training to a group of schools on a specific topic, which I have found extremely useful.
- Private educational psychologists are available for urgent work as they do not have to follow county protocols; they are quite expensive but many schools I visit are prepared to buy them in when necessary.

Cons:

- In areas where educational psychologists are scarce and cluster arrangements apply, it may be difficult to actually get an educational psychologist into your school unless it is for statutory work, such as EHCP reviews. My authority accepts consultations and reports as evidence of educational psychologist involvement but at times this is no real substitute for direct observation.
- If an educational psychologist feels they do not need to see a child, even for statutory work, it is very hard to obtain a positive outcome for the child.

SENDOs

Who are they?

Special educational needs and disability officers (SENDOs) work within the local authority and are based at the local area SEND office. Their role is to co-ordinate the statutory duties of the authority with regard to EHCP casework. They:

- Work in partnership with schools, families and other professionals in co-ordinating referrals and delivering outcomes tailored to the individual needs of the child.
- Draft high-quality EHCPs that accurately reflect the child's needs in line with statutory and legal requirements, as outlined in the SEND Code of Practice.
- Collate paperwork for SEND panels, funding requests and SEND tribunals.
- Consider applications for a change of setting, for example a request for specialist provision.
- Attend review meetings if asked (particularly where changes in funding are requested), including transition from primary to secondary school, for example.
- Attend co-production meetings with parents and schools (to look at the draft version) before the EHCP is finalised.

Case study 21

B had been awarded an EHCP for ASD/ADHD and the SENDO had emailed to ask whether the parent would attend a co-production meeting before the report was finalised. The parent agreed and during the course of the meeting, as well as editing changes, a number of school issues also emerged that were addressed straight away: B had one friend in school, whom he refused to engage with after a minor 'falling out' as he found it hard to 'let go' and so had no one to play with. School agreed to do some sessions on empathy and mediate with both children to try to resolve the issue. The SENDO agreed to amend the final paperwork in light of parental views.

Pros and cons

Pros:

- It is vital to develop a really positive relationship with your SENDO as they are the person who will help ensure that your paperwork is meeting all necessary criteria.
- The co-production meetings are really useful, so please ask for them.
- Try to follow SENDO advice where possible; there is a better chance of the referral being accepted by the panel (which is our key aim!).

Cons:

- It may take time to see your SENDO but it is better to wait than rush paperwork in.

Occupational therapists (OTs)

Who are they?

Community paediatric occupational therapists work for the NHS. Their role, according to NHS Greater Glasgow and Clyde (2018), is 'to provide intervention, support and/or advice to children and young people (0–18 years) and their families, where there is a disability or impairment which impacts on their performance and participation in everyday activities of life'. The aim is to enable children to effectively self-manage and become more independent. OTs liaise with children, families, educators and other professionals to support individual children with a programme of advice and activities. The children may:

- have poor gross and fine motor co-ordination skills
- have poor core stability
- have poor motor planning skills
- have visual perception/sensory difficulties.

As well as OTs giving advice to schools and providing programmes for schools to use, they will also, where appropriate, come into schools to deliver one-to-one support to the child. If a child requires an EHCP, they will provide medical advice to support an application for statementing.

Case study 22

Child G has cerebral palsy but has not currently got an EHCP, despite needing a wheelchair to be moved around the school, a standing frame for stretching, and a walker to move independently at play times; she also has a large pushchair for journeys to and from school and at lunchtimes to be moved across to the dining hall. G has OT input but school are currently awaiting updated input from OT and need EHCP funding to provide additional adult support to put in place the necessary programmes; sometimes G has to be carried to the toilet as she needs to go quickly, so there are some issues with moving and handling as one person is not enough to manage her needs (this is currently the class teaching assistant). G has a new therapist who has agreed to see her parent as soon as possible to give support at home, and to come into school to give further advice; she will also provide evidence that will hopefully support the EHCP referral.

Pros and cons

Pros:

- OTs are essential in helping children to make improvements in coping physically in their daily lives.

Cons:

- OTs are often over-stretched and can be hard to get hold of.
- OTs have not got the capacity to undertake one-to-one therapy unless the child has a disability that affects daily life significantly.
- Schools will try hard to put in place daily support using an OT's plan, but funding is needed to employ an extra adult to do this in cases such as G's in the case study.
- There can be long waiting lists for OT appointments.

Top tip

If you are awaiting the outcome of an OT referral and want some ideas for simple strategies to help the child improve, for example, holding a pencil, there is a really useful website called OT Plan (www.otplan.com), which is an activity and idea search engine that finds activities by skills and materials, and covers every area of need – brilliant! I have used it a lot and it's free.

School nurses

Who are they?

School nurses work for the NHS, working across education and health and linking school, health and the community. They work with families and children aged from five to 19 years and are usually linked with a group of schools. The website Health Careers (www.healthcareers.nhs.uk) describes the role of a school nurse: 'School nurses see all children with their parents during their first year of schooling for a health assessment, which will include a vision and hearing test.' Their day-to-day role includes:

- 'carrying out health assessments
- home visits to families in need
- providing health education, advice, and signposting to other sources of information [they can also refer in directly to community paediatrics]

- providing immunisation clinics
- advising and supporting schools with their public health agendas for example healthy eating advice, stop smoking programmes
- safeguarding and service co-ordination
- [advising] on common childhood conditions such as asthma, diabetes and eczema, working closely with general practitioners, health visitors and other health and social care staff' (Health Careers, 2015b).

Case study 23

L has complex needs, including autism, which is being investigated by SALT and the paediatrician. Although she has settled well into the school's reception class, her mother says her behaviours at home can be very difficult and she struggles to sleep. She displays a number of sensory issues, including pica and hypersensitivity to noise. She often has sensory overload in certain situations and has 'sensory meltdowns', which can be prolonged.

The school nurse was invited to a TAF meeting and was able to suggest some really useful ideas for both home and school; she also suggested useful referrals to external support services. Working collaboratively, we were all able to contribute positively to the TAF in order to support the child more effectively.

Pros and cons

Pros:

- The school nurse is an extremely valuable member of the support network, making a real difference to families and supporting the school with useful advice and practical solutions.

Cons:

- The school nurse can be hard to access at times, particularly if the caseload of schools is a large one.

Community paediatricians

Who are they?

Community paediatricians are doctors or consultants who undertake the assessment and treatment of children with a variety of developmental problems. The Community Children's Health Partnership (2013) explains their role and which children can be referred in to their service. Community paediatricians consider 'delayed milestones, learning difficulties, autism and cerebral palsy, and also children with behavioural problems including ADHD'. Categories can include:

- 'Impaired communication (including where Autistic Spectrum Disorder is suspected)
- Impaired motor function (e.g. Cerebral Palsy)
- Sensory impairment
- Impaired feeding
- Impaired sleep
- Impaired continence
- Impaired/restricted attention
- Developmental impairments
- Learning difficulties restricting access to learning activities or participation in school
- Prolonged absence from school on health grounds
- Epilepsy/possible seizures
- Chronic unexplained symptoms (e.g. pain, fatigue)
- Palliative care in life limiting conditions
- Children at risk of harm [in conjunction with Children's Social Care concerns]'.

Case study 24

Child K has complex needs surrounding his learning and behaviour and struggles to access an age-related curriculum; school suspect that there may be underlying medical issues that warrant further investigation. The parents are contacted, who then express concerns of their own; there are two potential paths they can go down – they can ask their family doctor to refer to a paediatrician or they can ask the school to refer in directly, with their permission. The parents go to their family doctor but ask school for a supporting statement outlining what they see. Child K is seen by a paediatrician, who sees his extreme impulsivity and lack of focus on learning as being potentially symptomatic of ADHD. The paediatrician sends out Conners forms (which are questionnaires that have a series of responses to questions to choose from; these are scored to see whether ADHD is indicated) and home and school responses dovetail with each other to indicate a high likelihood of ADHD; the parents are asked to consider medication, as the child's behaviours are extreme.

Pros and cons

Pros:

- As a SENCO I have found it to be important to be proactive in referring children in to the paediatric service to rule in or out underlying conditions, as these can play a major part in being a barrier to the child's learning.
- Good communication between all parties is the key to a successful collaboration.

Cons:

- There are often long waiting lists for referrals being accepted.
- There is not always a cohesive approach across the service to referrals; some will be accepted in some areas but not in others.

Clinical psychologists

Who are they?

Clinical psychologists work within the NHS; The School Run (2014) explains what the role entails. Clinical psychologists work in clinics 'similar to where GPs work'. They 'are interested in difficulties that children present that appear to be related to their life in general rather than specifically at school'. There will always be a thorough assessment, involving talking to the child, and subsequently, treatment could be 'individually with the child', where the clinical psychologist meets the child one to one, 'doing some therapy with drawing, playing or talking', or 'involving other people', for example sessions with the child's family. After this, it will then be decided what further interventions can be offered.

Case study 25

N was very emotional in school and at home and both the school and parents were concerned about his mental health and his ability to emotionally self-regulate. The school obtained some short-term counselling, which recommended some possible longer-term therapy. The school approached clinical psychology services, who said a CAF and TAF would have to be opened and Early Help Support Services accessed in the first instance. This was done and was deemed to be working successfully; clinical psychology would only be accessed if Early Help recommended that referral.

Top tip

If a child is referred into CAMHS and the threshold is not reached, then clinical psychology can be accessed with CAMHS passing on that referral.

Pros and cons

Pros:

- NICE (www.nice.org.uk) guidelines have to be followed and parents are usually required to attend or access some sort of parenting programme initially.

Cons:

- It is difficult to know which service can be accessed at what point, and can cause confusion as the thresholds are all different.
- It is important to check on current advice by contacting the relevant service directly – even GPs struggle with this!

Children and adolescent mental health services (CAMHS)

Who are they?

CAMHS work with children and young people who have difficulties with their emotional health and wellbeing. The NHS (2014) define CAMHS as:

> 'NHS mental health services that focus on the needs of children and young people. They are multidisciplinary teams that often consist of:
>
> - psychiatrists
> - psychologists
> - social workers
> - nurses
> - support workers
> - occupational therapists
> - psychological therapists – this may include child psychotherapists, family psychotherapists, play therapists and creative art therapists
> - primary mental health link workers
> - specialist substance misuse workers'.

CAMHS is usually a Tier 3 referral service (i.e. above Early Help and Wellbeing Services, which families can access initially). CAMHS referrals are governed by NICE guidelines so families are required to access external support services in the first instance. It is advisable to contact your local CAMHS office for further advice.

Case study 26

Child D was showing some mental health issues at the primary PRU, in the form of threats to self-harm and some actual self-harming incidents in the form of head banging and scratching. He was referred to CAMHS but did not meet the referral criteria as the self-harm incidents were not deemed to be serious. However, he subsequently tried to harm himself in a more serious way and was picked up by CAMHS after being rushed to hospital; he was then assessed, supported and alternative educational provision was found for him in a specialist placement near to home. As SENCO I was responsible for submitting the relevant paperwork.

Pros and cons

Pros:

- A successful referral means the child has access to a range of medical and other professionals, for example psychologists, ADHD specialists and other mental health specialists.

Cons:

- Early help services (Tier 2) need to be accessed first.
- The Tier 3 threshold is tricky to meet. A phone call to your local CAMHS department is worth making if you are unsure.

There are many other services you may wish to access, for example specialist teachers and a range of therapists, but these are the main professionals you can expect to regularly liaise with.

Chapter takeaways

- Update your contacts for professionals you regularly deal with and liaise with them regularly to support your SEND children.
- Research all supporting services in your area so that you have a thorough knowledge of available contacts and know how parents and families can be fully supported.

Chapter 9
Applying for statutory assessment: EHCPs

Applying for statutory assessment is such a vital part of the SENCO role, as it addresses the statutory needs of children in school with complex SEN. It rests with recognised needs in the areas of assess, plan, do and review and evidence has to be provided in order for a child's needs to be assessed carefully and properly (the graduated response). There are many reasons why your pupils may need EHCPs to support their complex needs but you need to ensure that you provide good supporting evidence. As long as you have robust whole-school systems in place to monitor SEN children's target-setting and progress, this should be quite straightforward; however, this is an area where many schools fall down as they haven't got a properly structured approach.

This chapter will be very focused on quoting from the SEND Code of Practice and related legislation, as the focus for many legal challenges from parents surrounds the request for an EHC needs assessment. As an outstanding SENCO, it is important that you refer closely to the legislation, in conjunction with seeking advice from the LEA SEN department; many complaints I hear from parents are that schools and SENCOs are ignorant of legislation and unwittingly carry out or collude with unlawful practices. You may be asked to support parents if an EHC needs assessment is turned down (schools cannot make this challenge) so it is vital to be au fait with statutory duties in order to point parents to the right help and support (information should be available on the LA Local Offer page on their website).

What is needed to apply for statutory assessment?

The SEND Code of Practice (Department for Education, 2014a, Section 6.63) says:

> 'SEN support should be adapted or replaced depending on how effective it has been in achieving the agreed outcomes. Where, despite the school having taken relevant and purposeful action to identify, assess and meet the SEN of the [child], the [child] has not made expected progress, the school or parents should consider requesting an Education, Health and Care needs assessment... To inform its decision the local authority will expect to see evidence of the action taken by the school as part of SEN support.'

Section 9 of the Code covers the key stages linked to statutory assessment; I will be referring to this statutory guidance but it needs to be looked at in depth by you as SENCO so that you are clear about what the process entails and can give proper information to parents in the first instance.

It is important to remember that a local authority has statutory 'must' duties in relation to carrying out a special needs assessment, to which it has to adhere. However, there are areas of the advice that are open to interpretation and often this is where problems can arise; I will discuss these later in the chapter, on page 118.

Who can ask for an assessment?

Section 9.8 of the Code of Practice states that the following have a specific right to ask the local authority to conduct an assessment:

- the child's parent
- a young person over 16 but under 25
- a person acting on behalf of a school.

The Code also states that anyone else can bring a child who has (or may have) SEN to the attention of the local authority, particularly where they think an EHC needs assessment may be necessary, for example:

- foster carers
- health and social care professionals
- Early Years practitioners.

There is advice for parents on how to apply and information about the processes on the Local Offer page on your local authority website.

It is worth iterating at this point that there is a legal test for local authorities, as stated in the Children and Families Act 2014, Section 36(8), and if a local authority is requested to carry out an EHC assessment of need by a parent, school or young person, they must consider:

- whether the child has, or may have, SEN
- whether they may need provision to be made through an EHCP.

'If the answer to both of these questions is yes, the local authority must carry out an EHC needs assessment.' (IPSEA, 2018) IPSEA has a model letter for a parent or young person to apply for an EHC assessment if school is not making the assessment. See www.ipsea.org.uk/making-a-request-for-an-ehc-needs-assessment.

The SEND Code of Practice (2014a, Section 9.14) says:

> 'In considering whether an EHC needs assessment is necessary, the local authority should consider whether there is evidence that despite the school having taken relevant, purposeful action to identify, assess and meet the special educational needs of the child, the child has not made expected progress. To inform their decision the local authority will need to take into account a wide range of evidence, and should pay particular attention to:
>
> - Evidence of the child's academic attainment (or developmental milestones in younger children) and rate of progress
> - Information about the nature, extent and context of the child's SEN
> - Evidence of the action already being taken by the school to meet the child's SEN

- Evidence that where progress has been made, it has only been as the result of much additional intervention and support over and above that which is usually provided
- Evidence of the child or young person's physical, social and emotional development and health needs, drawing on relevant evidence from clinicians and other health professionals and what has been done to meet these by other agencies.'

Top tip

It is useful to print out the criteria and keep it handy, as it will help you inform your application. The criteria should also be displayed on the Local Offer page of the LEA website.

In Section 9.16 of the Code it says:

> 'Local authorities may develop criteria as guidelines to help them decide when it is necessary to carry out an EHC needs assessment (and, following assessment, to decide whether it is necessary to issue an EHC Plan). However, local authorities must be prepared to depart from those criteria where there is compelling reason to do so in any particular case and demonstrate their willingness to do so where individual circumstances warrant such a departure.'

In some cases, there may be children who cannot be assessed under assess, plan, do, review, for instance children new to the country who have significant unmet needs that prevent them from accessing mainstream education. The LEA SEND department should be contacted immediately so that an appropriate assessment can be made of the child's individual circumstances.

This is a really tricky one... what is classed as 'compelling'? A recent example for me is a child from abroad with a diagnosis of complex needs but no further supporting evidence. Their request for an EHC needs assessment was turned down and now the school SENCO has to demonstrate two cycles of evidence to say the child cannot cope in a mainstream setting; she is aged six but can only manage in the nursery environment. Again, you will have to liaise with the LA SEND department on this; my advice is to follow their advice and do the best you can!

The time frames and actions for conducting an EHC needs assessment

Section 9.17 of the Code (2014a) says:

> 'The local authority must decide whether or not to proceed with an EHC needs assessment and must inform the child's parents and other relevant professionals of their decision within a maximum of six weeks from receiving a request for one, and must ensure that the parent is included from the start and given opportunities to offer views and information. If the LEA decides not to conduct an EHC needs assessment, it must inform the child's parents of their rights to appeal that decision and the time limit for doing so, of the requirement for them to consider mediation should they wish to appeal, and the availability of information, advice and support and disagreement resolution services. The local authority should also provide feedback collected during the process of considering whether an EHC needs assessment is necessary, including evidence from professionals, which the parent or school may find useful.'

So, as SENCO, when should you be considering an EHC needs assessment for a child with SEN? The referral criteria draws out key information indicating that if the child's needs are not being met without significant interventions from other sources, including medical or health professionals, educational psychologists, specialist teachers or additional one-to-one teaching assistant support, then this can be considered. This should be evidenced by assess, plan, do, review, known as the graduated response, and impact should be measured at each stage, usually over two cycles. Evidence can be in the form of educational psychologist reports, IEPs, provision maps, chronologies, medical and health reports, CAMHS reports, parent and child views, CAFs, TAFs, specialist teacher reports, Boxalls, and reports from other agencies such as Children's Social Care and the Virtual School.

Case study 27

A Year 4 pupil who is 'looked after' needs extra support over and above that which can be provided by the school. He has attachment issues and is displaying challenging behaviours at home with his foster carers and in school. He is very impulsive and will lash out at children who are 'in his space'. He is oppositional with adults and is not able to follow rules and boundaries; he has poor self-regulation skills and lacks empathy. He does not take responsibility for his own actions and struggles to make friendships with others. He is putting his own safety and that of others at risk and is in danger of exclusion. The Virtual School has agreed to put some funding in place for a limited amount of time for play therapy, an educational psychologist and some additional one-to-one teaching assistant support. A referral has also been made to the paediatrician to look at any possible underlying medical needs, for example ADHD (there is evidence that older siblings have received diagnoses for this). The school is evidencing assess, plan, do, review and will evaluate the impact of the additional interventions, which will be tailored to his individual needs. The SENDO will be consulted at an appropriate stage to assess the paperwork collated for an EHC needs assessment, which will then be submitted.

In relation to looked-after children, it is important to be aware of Section 9.38 of the Code (2014a):

> 'Local authorities should be particularly aware of the need to avoid any delays for looked after children and carry out the EHC needs assessment in the shortest possible timescale. Addressing a looked after child's special educational needs will be a crucial part of avoiding breakdown in their care placement.'

Completing the paperwork

There is no legal requirement to submit an application for an EHC needs assessment on any particular form of paperwork but in practice local authorities do have their own forms you will need to use to make applications; these can be found on your local authority Local Offer website.

The forms will usually ask for evidence of strengths and needs in the following areas:

- cognition and learning
- communication and interaction
- social, emotional and mental health (SEMH)
- physical and sensory needs
- independence and self-help.

These broad headings cover the criteria that the local authority is able to apply on deciding whether to carry out an EHC needs assessment and it is important to consult with the LA SEND to see what is required. However, it may be that even if the assessment goes forward it will not necessarily mean an EHCP will be issued.

Timescales

So what are the timescales for this process? Unless there are exceptional circumstances, these are as follows (see Section 9.41 of the Code, 2014a):

- 'Local authorities must give their decision in response to any request for an EHC needs assessment within a maximum of six weeks from when the request was received or the point at which a child was brought to the local authority's attention
- When local authorities request information as part of the EHC needs assessment process, those supplying the information must respond in a timely manner and within a maximum of six weeks from the date of the request
- If a local authority decides, following an EHC needs assessment, not to issue an EHCP, it must inform the child's parents within a maximum of 16 weeks from the date of request
- The child's parents must be given 15 calendar days to consider and provide views on a draft EHC Plan and ask for a particular school or other institution to be named in it [a co-production meeting is often arranged between the parent and the SENDO to discuss this]
- The maximum time for the whole process to be completed is 20 weeks, including the final Plan'.

What to expect from an EHCP

If an EHCP is issued following the EHC needs assessment, it is important as SENCO to know what you can expect from the plan. Section 9.61 of the Code states that the plan should:

- Include evidence that the plan has been produced collaboratively with parents, children and relevant professionals. Parent and pupil voice should be an inherent part of the plan.
- Reflect the positive achievements of children as well as outlining needs, and should be written in a clear, consistent and jargon-free format, which is understandable to all.
- Include clear guidance on how outcomes will be met for the child, and targets should be SMART (specific, measurable, achievable, realistic, time-bound).
- Be clear about how the child will be supported by their family and community as well as professionals in meeting the needs of the child.
- Reflect movement towards important transition milestones, for example Key Stage 1 to Key Stage 2, and support this process.

Section 9.62 of the Code states that the format for an EHCP can be agreed locally, so they will differ depending on your local authority, but as a 'statutory minimum' EHCPs must include the following sections:

Section A: The views, interests and aspirations of the child and his or her parents.

Section B: The child's special educational needs.

Section C: The child's health needs relevant to their SEN.

Section D: The child's social care needs relevant to their SEN or to a disability.

Section E: The outcomes sought for the child. The plan should identify short-term targets by the school or other provider.

Section F: The special educational provision required by the child.

Section G: Any health provision reasonably required by the learning difficulties or disabilities that result in the child having SEN. Where an Individual Health Care Plan is made for them, that plan should be included.

Section H1: Any social care provision that must be made for a child under 18 resulting from Section 2 of the Chronically Sick and Disabled Persons Act 1970.

Section H2: Any other social care provision reasonably required by the learning difficulties or disabilities that result in the child having SEN.

Section I: The name and type of school to be attended by the child.

Section J: Details of a personal budget (if that has been requested; see page 125).

Section K: The advice and information gathered during the EHC needs assessment must be attached (in appendices). There should be a list of this advice and information.

Source: Department for Education, 2014a

In Section 9.69 of the Code, there is an exemplar of the information to be provided in each of the above sections. There is also a section on agreed responsibility between education, health and social care needs on what is to be included in the plan.

The draft EHCP

When the draft plan is issued, the child and parents must be given at least 15 days to give their views and the local authority should make an officer (SENDO) available to meet with parents if requested. The draft plan will not name a school but parents should be given a list of schools available for their child to attend. The parent can request that a particular school be named in the plan; however, there is a rider to this (see Section 9.79): the school must be named in the plan, unless:

- 'it would be unsuitable for the age, ability, aptitude or SEN of the child'
- 'the attendance of the [child] there would be incompatible with the efficient education of others, or the efficient use of resources'.

This second point refers to parents requesting mainstream provision, as schools must demonstrate that they can take reasonable steps to ensure that admitting the child would not be incompatible with the efficient education of other pupils. Section 9.91 illustrates what constitutes 'reasonable steps' – for example, would this be compatible with what the setting could provide and the effectiveness with which needs could be met? Also, what are the resource implications for the school and what disruption may occur if the school took the steps? Section 9.92 gives some examples, including having sufficient plans in place to meet the child's needs, including positive handling plans. Section 9.94 says:

> 'A decision not to educate a child in a mainstream setting against the wishes of a child's parent is not to be taken lightly. It is important that all decisions are taken on the basis of the circumstances of each case and in consultation with parents, taking account of the child's views… reasonable steps should be taken to provide for children with SEN and disabled children.'

However the Code of Practice does not specify what it means by 'the efficient use of resources'; in my experience, that usually means any specialist provision that is not local to where the child lives (which impinges on transport costs for the authority) or where the provider is privately commissioned, rather than being 'county' provision. In Section 9.84 the Code states:

> 'The child's parent… may also make representations for places in non-maintained [schools and] the local authority must have regard to the general principle in section 9 of the Education Act 1996 that children should be educated in accordance with their parents' wishes, so long as this is compatible with the provision of efficient instruction and training and does not mean unreasonable public expenditure.'

These are the grey areas that inform the basis of appeals, which I will look at on page 128; at the time of writing, the government is looking to inject extra funding into local authority SEND budgets – whether this will be sufficient remains to be seen.

If no request for a particular school is made, a mainstream primary will be specified unless it is against the parent's wishes or incompatible with the efficient education of others.

Case study 28

A school has applied for an EHC assessment of needs for a Year 6 child, which has resulted in a draft EHCP and, through a co-production meeting, next steps have been discussed at length with the parent. The parent feels that she wants her child to attend a mainstream secondary school but the child is indicating that she is finding mainstream primary a struggle, despite the reasonable steps taken by school to provide an environment suited to her individual, complex needs. Eventually it is agreed that the child will attend mainstream secondary school with a carefully tailored transition plan in place to support her; the secondary school say they can meet her needs and will ensure that provision is regularly reviewed. The Year 6 teacher will make sure that the final EHCP is annotated as a working document with strategies and provision that work for the child, and the SENCO will liaise with the secondary school SENCO to revise the plan where necessary in the summer term.

Top tip

I think it is important not to assume that a child will struggle at secondary school just because they are finding primary school difficult at times. Many of my specialist teacher friends say that some children, often on the autistic spectrum, actually find mainstream secondary school more accessible than their primary schools if the right support is in place, as they like the increased routines and the teachers linked to specific subjects; it is important not to generalise but look at the individual picture for a specific child!

Personal budgets

So what is a personal budget? In my experience, these are rare at primary schools because parents accept that the school is already paying for support out of the school budget, and have often done this without the child accessing an EHC needs assessment; however, it is an area you need to be aware of.

The Code of Practice (Section 9.95) defines a personal budget as 'an amount of money identified by the local authority to deliver provision set out in an EHCP where the parent is involved in securing that provision'.

Personal budgets are optional but there is a requirement for local authorities to provide information and costings when requested; they are designed to secure the outcomes in the plan. It is rare in primary for parents to request a personal budget as this would be taken out of the school budget monies arising from the plan. If a child is receiving high one-to-one adult support in school, it would make no sense for a parent to ask for the money for something else as the support could not then be funded. In older children where one-to-one support is not provided or needed, a personal budget could cover assistive technology or particular therapies, for example. It is worth parents consulting SENDIASS services if they are unsure about whether to claim.

Finalising and maintaining the EHCP

Any amendments to the final plan can only arise after consultation with the parent at the draft stage. If these are not agreed, the parent may appeal to a tribunal and they should be notified of the time limit for doing so. The child's parent can appeal to the tribunal about the description of SEND in the plan, the provision named for that and the school, which may be named or not named.

Reviewing an EHCP

EHCPs should be reviewed on an annual basis. Reviews must focus on the child's progress towards achieving the outcomes specified in the plan. The review needs to consider whether the outcomes and targets are appropriate (see 9.166 for further information) and what changes (if any) need to be made.

The SENCO and class teacher should review all the targets set out in the plan and review how much progress has been made by the pupil; some targets may need tweaking or changing. For example, if a child has moved into Key Stage 2, the targets will generally specify what needs to have been achieved by the end of Key Stage 1, so targets for Key Stage 2 should be set. Obviously, if these need to be 'rolled over' due to still being ongoing, that is fine, but further amendments can be made each year up until the end of Key Stage 2 to reflect ongoing progress over the key stage. At the end of Key Stage 2, the secondary school SENCO will need to be involved in the Year 6 annual review. At a recent review I conducted, the secondary school SENCO said she would re-set Key Stage 3 targets two months into the new term, but check with your SEND department what their practice is.

It should also be considered whether the plan needs to be kept or not – the latter is highly unlikely in primary provision. The local authority will have specific review paperwork on their Local Offer for reviews, which includes collecting pupil and parent voice; the views of other professionals may also be sought and the school will be asked for updated advice. As well as an annual review, there is also the facility to hold an emergency review if circumstances change significantly, e.g. if a possible move to specialist provision is to be considered. Under these circumstances, the school EP should be consulted and the SENDCO should be invited to the review.

Case study 29

Child T had his annual review in the summer of his Year 2 placement. At the review his parent articulated that she thought he was doing well in school, in line with a highly differentiated personalised curriculum, although her main concern was that he had friends and close relatives in school who supported him and she wanted him to be in a mainstream setting. In the autumn term, he was clearly distressed about being in a Key Stage 2 class, not because his work was not being differentiated, but because the transition was affecting him more than either the school or his parent envisaged. The parent asked for an emergency meeting and said she wanted specialist provision for him; this was under review procedures but the outcome was not certain – the school had to demonstrate how they were not meeting his needs, and support needs were required from evidence of the assess, plan, do, review process.

An emergency review was called, with the local authority SENDO and educational psychologist in attendance, and evidence was presented by the school, the parent and the child. The parent was accompanied by an independent LEA supporter (SENDIASS). At the time of writing, the school is awaiting the outcome. If the request is turned down then the parent will appeal.

Appeals

How does the appeals process work? For this, it is worth having a closer look at the legislation contained in the Children and Families Act (UK Government, 2014b). Section 19(d) clearly states that 'a local authority must have regard to the following: the need to support the child and his or her parent in order to facilitate the development of the child and help him or her achieve the best possible education and other outcomes'.

It also states:

> '20 (1) A child has special educational needs if he or she has a learning difficulty or disability which calls for special educational provision to be made for him or her
>
> 20 (2) A child of compulsory school age has a learning difficulty or disability if she or he (a) has a significantly greater difficulty in learning than the majority of others of the same age, or
>
> (b) has a disability which prevents or hinders him of her from making use of facilities of a kind generally provided for others of the same age in mainstream schools'.

The above criteria are particularly significant when it comes to an application for an EHC needs assessment, and appeals often arise when this is refused. As discussed earlier, an authority only needs to look at whether a child may have special needs and may need an EHCP in order to start the process.

A specific example of this can be found on www.gov.uk by searching for RB v Calderdale MBC (SEN). It is well worth reading the full Upper Tribunal judgement, which overturns the First-Tier Tribunal SEND decision in January 2018, which found against the appellant (parent). The basis of the appeal was that RB had a chronic health condition that led to long absences from school and the parent requested an EHC needs assessment as these were a barrier to his learning. The local authority and First-Tier Tribunal found against RB as he was academically bright and required a health needs assessment only. The parent argued that this was insufficient and that there were adjustments that could be specified via an EHCP such as home tutoring for times when he was really poorly. The conclusions of the Upper Tribunal were that the initial Tribunal involved a material error of law, namely that it asked the wrong question in looking at whether RB did need an EHC needs assessment as opposed to may need an assessment.

Sections 21 and 22 say:

> 'The Tribunal appear to be equating the type of support R might need with the sort of "catch-up" assistance provided to a pupil with no disability or learning difficulty who misses a few days of school because of a nasty virus… [It] failed to give sufficient weight to the fact that R was not at school... and failed to consider what provision might be necessary to ensure that he was able to return to school. As such, the Tribunal missed the point that the interventions R required to enable him to return to (and remain at) school (e.g. home tuition and help to address the mental health issues associated with his physical disability) delivered "otherwise than at a school", "might" have fallen within the definition of special educational provision.'

Conclusion and disposal:

> '23. For all the reasons explained above, R's appeal against the decision of the First-Tier Tribunal succeeds. The Tribunal's decision involves a material error of law. I therefore set aside the decision of the First-Tier Tribunal and by consent order as follows:
>
> 1. Pursuant to section 12(2)(a) of the Tribunals, Courts and Enforcement Act 2007, the decision of the First-Tier Tribunal (SEND), taken on 10 January 2018… involves an error of law and is set aside.'

Parts 2 and 3 state that an EHC needs assessment must be completed within ten weeks and a decision given to parents in that timescale. If an EHCP is agreed it must be issued within 14 weeks of the order. The young person must not be identified as a result of this appeal.

I feel it is important to give this example at length as it is important for you, as an outstanding SENCO, to realise that the law trumps all, and no local authority or First-Tier Tribunal is infallible. The child is central to all decisions made, whatever the level of professional input, and parents need support from you as they are vulnerable to wider legal challenges from authorities who may have more resources available to them; in this case, RB's parent secured what she needed but many more parents lack the resilience or capability to act alone. It is extremely important for you to signpost all relevant agencies who can help them mount a legal challenge, where necessary, and provide supporting evidence where and when requested.

The Act Section 51 specifies the circumstances in which parents can appeal to the First-Tier Tribunal, subject to section 55 (mediation):

> 'The matters are—
>
> (a) a decision of a local authority not to secure an EHC needs assessment for the child;
> (b) a decision of a local authority, following an EHC needs assessment, that it is not necessary for special educational provision to be made for the child in accordance with an EHC plan;
> (c) where an EHCP is maintained for the child or young person—
>   (1) the child's special educational needs as specified in the plan;
>   (2) the special educational provision as specified in the plan;
>   (3) the school or type of school named in the plan;
>   (4) if no school is named in the plan;
> (d) a decision of a local authority not to secure a re-assessment of the needs of a child under section 44 if requested to do so;
> (e) a decision of a local authority not to secure the amendment or replacement of an EHC Plan it maintains for the child following a review or assessment under section 44;
> (f) a decision of a local authority under section 45 to cease to maintain an EHCP for the child or young person.
> (3) A child's parent... may appeal to the First-Tier Tribunal under subsection (2)(c)—
> (a) when an EHC Plan is first finalized for the child or young person, and
> (b) following an amendment or replacement of the plan.'

Right to mediation

The right to mediation applies where an appeal may be brought under the above criteria and must be undertaken by an independent adviser, i.e. someone who is not employed by a commissioning authority or group; disagreement resolution features prominently in the Children and Families Act 2014. It is a service that only parents/carers are entitled to access; for more information see The Special Educational Needs (Mediation) Regulations (https://assets.publishing.service.gov.uk/government/uploads/system/uploads/attachment_data/file/251853/Consultation_on_draft_0_to_25_Special_Educational_Needs__SEN__-_mediation_regulations.pdf). Further advice on how to gain mediation/advocacy that represents parents' views can be sought from the LA and will be linked into the Local Offer page on the LA website.

To sum up, the only right of appeal comes from parents but you as SENCO can support your parents when called on to do so; further supporting evidence may be requested from you if there is an appeal, and you cannot underestimate how this help will be positively received by members of your school community. Good luck!

Chapter takeaways

- Have a read of any case law examples, for example the RB v Calderdale case, and link these to any cases you may be dealing with (see www.gov.uk/administrative-appeals-tribunal-decisions/rb-v-calderdale-mbc-sen-2018-ukut-390-aac).
- Consider accessing legal training from a reputable provider, for example IPSEA. This will give you a whole new perspective on legal entitlements; bonus points if you can include your headteacher!

Chapter 10
Accountability: data and an evidence-based approach

The assessment of progress made by pupils with SEND can take a number of forms and should be both summative and formative. It should sit within a framework of a robust whole-school approach to target setting and tracking, with regular pupil progress meetings that highlight any child who is underachieving or making insufficient progress in their learning; this obviously needs unpicking as the child may have SEN, despite good quality-first teaching and appropriate differentiation. The 'assess' part of the SEND Code of Practice (Department for Education, 2014a) highlights sources of information to be used in building a picture of a pupil's strengths and needs, such as teacher assessment and experience, previous progress and attainment, and parental and pupil views. If specialists or other professionals from health and social care are involved, their views should be taken into account in informing assessments; if not, as SENCO you may wish to contact specialists to pinpoint exactly where a child's needs may lie.

It may be that specific assessment 'tools' are needed to give a clearer picture, for example standardised tests, profiling tools (such as for speech, language and communication needs or behaviour), assessments that are criterion-referenced (part of teacher assessment), screening tests (such as dyslexia and SALT assessments), observations or specialist teacher reports of assessments they have made. Targeted provision can then be planned for at the 'plan' stage and clear and expected outcomes can be put in place to measure the success or otherwise of a particular intervention.

Formative assessment

Formative assessment is assessment for learning (AfL); it gives a picture of the child's strengths and needs and which approaches work best for the child. This information is crucial for identifying suitable interventions and provision. AfL refers to the approaches used in gathering evidence about a pupil's learning. Teachers can do this by:

- observing
- listening
- discussing
- questioning
- reviewing work in progress.

The child is active in assessing his or her own learning and works in partnership with the teacher and other adults, such as support staff, to develop next steps. It has an immediate impact as the teacher can adjust teaching approaches lesson by lesson to improve the learning for the pupil.

Case study 30

When I was at the PRU, teaching children with complex behavioural and SEN needs, I found AfL strategies invaluable in informing my planning on a daily basis and they gave me and other adults a deeper understanding of the child's strengths and needs. I always had a working wall for English and maths and relevant strategies, often from 'work in progress' rather than manicured displays, and children and adults would use sticky notes to ask questions, practise skills, highlight gaps that needed closing and show current learning. This individual approach was great for enhancing the child's self-esteem and making them feel 'included' in assessing their own learning needs and developing skills; it also felt less 'threatening' to them than traditional teaching approaches (namely whole-class instruction), which they had often failed to engage with. The adults (teacher and teaching assistant) could immediately see what needed changing and why and have a joint approach in supporting the pupil. Of course, other approaches (including whole-class approaches) were used but the AfL was precious as the children were given an individual voice.

For more information on formative assessment, see the Council for the Curriculum, Examinations and Assessment webpage on formative assessment and AfL, which lists useful, up-to-date resources for further reading: http://ccea.org.uk/curriculum/assess_progress/types_assessment/formative/assessment_learning.

Summative assessment

Summative assessment is the more formal summing-up of a child's progress, such as the phonics screening check in Year 1, Key Stage 1 SATs in Year 2 and Key Stage 2 SATs in Year 6. In primary schools, formal assessments often take place through the year as part of the whole-school target-setting and progress review process for each child. This gives valuable insight into what a child does or does not know, showing where understanding is insecure. It can be linked to formative assessment by involving the child in reviewing their own progress over a set period of time and helping teachers evaluate their own practice. In this way, summative assessment can be diagnostic in flagging up a pupil's future needs. It is also evaluative as it ensures that there is appropriate accountability throughout school and it informs curriculum planning and monitoring procedures.

However, whole-school summative assessments can be too broad-brush for some pupils with SEN who are making very small steps of progress. There are a number of commercial programmes that help schools to do this and many schools with specialist provision use these to accurately track progress.

I am going to focus on the ones I am most familiar with, but if you need something to be in place at your school that is not just about meeting age-related expectations, ask around at your local cluster meetings or nearby schools for recommendations.

P scales

Following the Rochford Review consultation in 2017 (search the www.gov.uk website for Rochford Review: final report), the Standards and Testing Agency (STA) published the new pre-key stage standards at Key Stage 1 and Key Stage 2 for use from the 2018/19 academic year.

Pre-key stage standards are for pupils who are working below the overall standard of National Curriculum assessments, but who are engaged in subject-specific study and are above P scales one to four.

So what are these standards? At Key Stage 1 there are four standards (these replace P scales) that are used to make statutory teacher assessment judgements in aspects of reading, writing and maths, based on evidence from the child's daily work. There is no requirement that a portfolio of evidence be kept and it is not a formative assessment tool; it is purely for summative assessment at the end of the key stage. At Key Stage 2 there are six standards that are used to make statutory teacher assessment judgements in respect of reading, writing and maths; again it is purely for summative assessment at the end of the key stage.

In both cases, these are not intended to replace in-depth assessments of other curricular areas, in line with whole-school assessment procedures, or be used for assess, plan, do, review according to the SEN Code of Practice.

Full guidance can be found in the following documents:

- '2018 to 2019 pre-key stage 1: pupils working below the national curriculum assessment standard': www.gov.uk/government/publications/pre-key-stage-1-standards
- '2018 to 2019 pre-key stage 2: pupils working below the national curriculum assessment standard': www.gov.uk/government/publications/pre-key-stage-2-standards

Top tip

It is worth exploring what the Rochford Review (search the www.gov.uk website for Rochford Review: final report) covered and the government response to the review in 2017 to understand the background to these changes. There are some very interesting ideas surrounding areas of engagement that mirror the kinds of approaches common in EYFS assessment.

PIVATS and other tracking systems

PIVATS are Performance Indicators for Valued Assessment and Targeted Learning; for more information see www.lancashire.gov.uk/pivats.

So what are they? PIVATS provides a structured approach to assessing, planning, tracking and measuring small steps of progress, focusing on steps within the P scales (1 to 4) going up to revised National Curriculum Year 4 age-related expectations.

I have used PIVATS extensively across many schools and it does what it says on the tin; it is a commercial scheme, but many schools I know feel it is worth buying into as it does indeed measure small steps of progress. There is a certain amount of subjectivity looking at 'best fit' for the child using some of the targets, so it is useful to look at them with another colleague who knows the child well. The scheme is available on DVD and easy to use; it covers reading, writing and maths and there is a separate DVD coming soon for personal and social development (PSED Toolkit). There is also an online assessment and tracking tool that measures progress for individual pupils across time.

There is a range of other commercial computerised tracking systems available, for example ProvisionMap (see www.provisionmap.co.uk), which maps out interventions and keeps track of them, generating reports for school and parents. Many whole-school tracking systems allow you as SENCO to separately analyse the data collected for children with SEN and input targets; this is useful but putting it into a whole-school context means that other children who are struggling to meet their targets get early identification if they need to be on the SEN register at SEN support. It also means that SEN children on pupil premium are being monitored for both strands and is useful for directing how pupil premium money could be spent in meeting their needs. CPOMS is a commercial software application for monitoring child protection, safeguarding, special educational needs and other areas that can inform chronologies for individual children (see www.cpoms.co.uk).

In practice, tracking systems will be put in place by school leaders, so you as a SENCO may not have much choice over what to use in your school; however, I would advise against setting up time-consuming spreadsheets inputted by you alone as this will take up a great deal of your time, which could be better spent with children! If PIVATS are used for those children working below National Curriculum levels in conjunction with the school tracker, that should be enough to give a clear picture of a child's achievements and information can be shared with all staff at regular pupil progress meetings. It also means that senior leaders are aware at all times of the progress of children with SEN. One school

I worked in had a tracker devised by the SENCO that was not shared with staff or senior leaders, and when the SENCO left it remained half-finished on her desktop! This does not help accountability!

Of course, underpinning tracking are the interventions and assessments referred to earlier in Chapter 7, which inform expected individual progress.

Interventions

Individual or small-group interventions will arise at the 'assess' part of the process. What does the child need? Schools often already have interventions in place as part of whole-school provision mapping and these may be linked to reading, spelling, maths, writing or phonics, so unless there is a specific difficulty that is not being covered, it may mean that expertise within school has already been sourced. It is the responsibility of the class teacher to oversee provision maps for their SEND pupils, not yours as SENCO. However, you need to have the school or class plan to check that the SEN pupils are being correctly provided for; targets linked to these should also be on the child's IEP or learning plan.

Try not to be drawn into costing everything to the nth degree as this is a waste of your valuable time; as long as you have an overview of costs linked to value for money and effectiveness, for example if a specialist teacher is involved, a child is in a regular phonics group or you are buying into a specialist dyslexia scheme like Nessy Reading and Writing, that is sufficient. Also there is often an overlap with other subject leaders, for example Read Write Inc may have an intensive monitoring process undertaken by the English or phonics lead. Likewise, pupil premium funding linked to outcomes will be monitored by that lead person. The assessment co-ordinator will oversee all assessment in school, of which pupils with SEN are part. It is more important to liaise with these colleagues to get a holistic view of the impact of extra provision, rather than (in my opinion) work out the monetary worth of half an hour's reading catch-up three times a week. Don't forget your time also needs to be costed out and needs to be an efficient use of resources.

Cognitive tests

There may be times when you need to have a deeper insight into the extent of a child's difficulties and cognitive testing is a useful tool for gaining this. There are a range of commercial tests on the market that can be administered either in-house or by a specialist, for example a specialist teacher or an educational psychologist.

Standardised tests require all pupils to answer the same questions in the same way and are non-subjective. They are scored in a way that allows schools to compare the relative performance of the pupils; they are often administered for baseline purposes or at key points when a child is making insufficient progress, despite a differentiated, individualised programme of support. The tests produce raw scores that are converted into standardised age scores (SAS) that measure performance against a national sample of pupils of the same age (in years and months). The average score is 100 so anything above or below is above or below average. The national percentile rank (NPR) relates to the SAS score and shows the percentage of pupils obtaining a particular score. An NPR of 5 shows a pupil is in the lowest five per cent of the sample; an NPR of 95 shows the pupil is in the highest five per cent of the sample. These are not infallible (the same is true of any form of testing); however, for SEN purposes, where a child is experiencing significant difficulties, they can inform planning for individual or small-group interventions and provide evidence towards an EHC needs assessment. For more information see www.edglossary.org/standardized-test.

Example cognitive tests

The following examples are not exhaustive; again it is useful to ask around to see which ones may be useful in your school and give value for money. If you are engaging specialists to undertake the work, it is useful to have some understanding of the nature of the assessments they are conducting.

Tests administered in school (class/groups/individuals) could include:

- NFER (www.nfer.ac.uk) tests in a range of areas – reading, maths, grammar and punctuation, spelling.

- Rising Stars (see www.risingstars-uk.com) have a range of progress tests across Key Stages 1 and 2.

More specialised assessments include:

- The British Picture Vocabulary Scale (BPVS) is a non-reading test useful for speech and language therapists and assesses a child's receptive language; it can be useful in school to inform referrals to that service. (For more information see www.gl-assessment.co.uk.)
- The Renfrew Language Scales assessment (for children aged three to eight years) is conducted on a one-to-one basis and is an action picture test, useful if a child has difficulties with expressive language (see soundingboard.earfoundation.org.uk).
- The Salford Reading Test is carried out one to one and standardised for primary-age pupils; it is a sentence reading test that can be used for miscue analysis (see www.hoddereducation.co.uk).
- York Assessment of Reading for Comprehension (YARC) is a reading test with individual computerised score sheets that measures reading ability (see www.gl-assessment.co.uk).
- The Test of Word Reading Efficiency (TOWRE2) has a non-reading and a real-reading section and gives a standardised score of their efficiency; it is one to one, quick and easy to use, and suitable for primary-age children (see www.pearsonclinical.co.uk).
- WRAT-4 and WRAT-5 accurately measure word and sentence reading and comprehension, spelling and maths computation (see www.pearsonclinical.co.uk).
- The Sandwell Early Numeracy Test (SENT) assesses early maths skills for primary-age children (see https://gl-education.com/products/sandwell-early-numeracy-test-sent).
- Working Memory Rating Scale (WMRS) is a rating scale that identifies children with working memory deficits. It is suitable for children aged five to 11 years (see www.pearsonclinical.co.uk).

In Chapter 7, page 92, I talked about interventions for children with SEMH and the use of the Boxall Profile. Many primary schools have formal or informal nurture provision for their most vulnerable children and Boxall is a useful tool to measure progress in 'closing gaps' for children with significant SEMH issues, such as attachment. You can set a baseline and then reassess at regular intervals – half-termly or termly – to see whether the work done with the child has had any impact (see Beyond the Boxall for suggestions for activities matched to the child's identified needs). Full information and a range of useful articles and resources can be found on www.nurtureuk.org. The Boxall Profile, both paper copies and a computerised assessment program, and Beyond the Boxall are available to purchase from the website.

As I have said, this is not an exhaustive list but will hopefully give you a starting point to look at the range of assessments that are out there. It is important to decide whether you, as SENCO, plan to routinely undertake some one-to-one assessments, for example using WRAT-4, but be aware that these can be time-consuming and have cost implications. If you are fortunate in having a non-teaching role, it may be worthwhile conducting some in-house assessments as part of assess, plan, do, review. However, if you know you will not have the time, it may be worth buying in specialists as and when needed. In one of my schools I keep hold of the Nessy screeners (for possible dyslexia) but class teachers use and monitor the Nessy Reading and Spelling to measure steps of progress for children with SEN in their classes; this is delivered by support staff in small intervention groups, but the children go at their own pace, so it is really a case of keeping children on task and encouraging them to try their best.

Chapter takeaways

- Look at the children on your SEN register and match their needs up with the interventions that are supporting them in school – is anything more needed or possible?
- Consider whether there are any new interventions or assessments that could usefully support the needs of your SEN children. Speak to other SENCOs or talk to SEN advisers in your LEA; at one cluster meeting we started a database of the most useful interventions and standardised assessments available.

Chapter 11
Promoting wellbeing and managing your own work–life balance

It is important that as well as promoting wellbeing amongst children and staff, you look after your own wellbeing and work–life balance. Being a SENCO is a demanding role and if you have too many areas competing for your attention this can cause a problem. Many SENCOs I have supported, for instance, have significant class teaching or management roles that impinge on SENCO time and can lead to a feeling of not doing the job well or an inability to cope.

In this chapter I am going to look at how, as a SENCO, you can support the wellbeing of children with SEN, parents who may find their child's needs overwhelming at times and colleagues who may be struggling to support SEN children, particularly if the pupil has challenging behaviours, all without neglecting your own needs in the process.

When I was at the PRU, it really came home to me how children's complex needs, including severe behavioural difficulties, impact on those around them – at home, in school and in the local community. As a staff we were fortunate in having a lot of support and training around containment and we had some brilliant CPD on the Solihull Approach, which is for parents and professionals (see https://solihullapproachparenting.com). This is a holistic programme that covers the themes of containment, reciprocity and behaviour management as a way of focusing on relationships in a calm and positive manner and building resilience.

Top tip

A really useful read is a PowerPoint that explains the Solihull Approach in detail; it can be found on www.lancashirechildrenstrust.org.uk/news/index.asp?articles=73797. It talks about brain development and attachment theory, which underpin the approach.

Containment is the ability to communicate with others without feeling overwhelmed. When we are 'full up' with our own problems and issues, we have little left to give to others, and understanding this can help us as professionals understand and recognise our limitations. Reciprocity is about building positive reciprocal relationships between adults and adults, adults and children, and children and children. These are key in informing behaviour management techniques, which teach a child self-control and facilitate learning and development.

Obviously this training comes at a cost, but the principles are well worth pondering on as they may help you put your SENCO role in context when working with stakeholders. It is important that you are working as part of a team and are not left alone to deal with issues that are draining you. I have been in many meetings that are stressful and in situations where pupils are 'out of control' and we need to ensure that there is an element of supervision so that we can 'debrief' ourselves and for others to regain appropriate containment. For this to happen, it needs to be integral to whole-school procedures and accessible to those that need it, whether it be a child, a parent, a colleague or yourself.

Supporting pupils with SEN

In school all children need the support of the school community, but children with SEN are particularly vulnerable; most of the children I work with have extreme anxiety at the heart of their needs, which can lead to mental health issues if not addressed. If reasonable adjustments are in place to support a pupil's SEN this will go a long way to enhancing wellbeing and increasing resilience.

So how can we recognise when a child is struggling with anxiety? Some signs to look out for are:

- poor sleeping patterns
- poor eating
- finding it hard to concentrate and being fidgety or impulsive
- complaining of tummy aches or feeling unwell generally
- crying, being clingy or showing separation anxiety from a parent
- wanting to go to the toilet often and staying there for long periods of time (often a work-avoidance issue linked to their unmet needs)
- appearing worried or anxious or showing anger or irritability
- not wanting to come to school
- becoming distressed by small things, being obsessive
- having 'meltdowns' (which could be due to sensory overload) and struggling to calm down; in extreme cases the child may destroy property or attack other pupils and adults
- self-harming behaviours such as biting, intense scratching, head banging or hitting.

It is obviously important to discuss these with parents to see whether they have noticed any changes in their child's behaviour at home and to work out what might be at the root of the anxiety. In most cases, I would recommend that the parent take their child to the doctor to check out whether there are any underlying medical issues; it may be that a referral on to a paediatrician is needed to rule in or out any possible other needs, such as ADHD or ASC. Talk to the class teacher and other adults who work closely with the child; often they can pinpoint areas where the child is struggling. If there is a family support worker or learning mentor in school, they are often trusted adults that the child is comfortable talking to and they may be able to unpick worries or problems. Talk to the child yourself and see whether there is anything that could help them; do not push if they are unwilling or unable to say what is worrying them but attempt to come up with some simple things to try. These could include:

- One-to-one sessions in a quiet room with the child completing a favoured activity such as colouring or playing a shared game. (These could be with the teaching assistant, family support worker or learning mentor.)
- Discussing with the teacher differentiated approaches to learning and what support the child is getting in class; simple tweaking can mean that a child immediately feels less anxious if they are presented with tasks that seem 'easier'.
- Engaging a specialist teacher to do some work on emotions and give strategies for the child to self-manage and self-regulate (in more complex cases); they can also feed back to the adults working with the child, including you as SENCO, and suggest further strategies for the assess, plan, do, review process.
- Looking more closely at unstructured times, for example playtimes or lunchtimes; these are often difficult for children with underlying needs, such as ADHD, ASD or SPD.

In and out of class, look at simple adjustments that could help the child:

1. Allocate the child an older 'buddy' to help him or her cope with social situations they may find tricky and to model appropriate behaviour.
2. Provide ear defenders if noise sensitivity is an issue.
3. Look at transition points, for example moving from the playground into a crowded, noisy cloakroom.
4. Allocate an adult to help the child cope, for example in lunchtime clubs and activity or friendship groups (inside and outside).
5. Look at the classroom environment; does the child need to be provided with an individual workstation if they are distractible or distracting others? Being impulsive or unable to concentrate can be very stressful for the child and everyone else in class, so it makes sense to provide them with a calm space in which to work. The workstation can be personalised with a visual timetable (a child with ADHD or ASC can become very anxious if change is not signposted in advance, so knowing what will be happening

in the day can reduce anxiety for these pupils) and a box of independent activities, 'now and next' cards and timers.

6. Provide a safe space outside the classroom for when a child is becoming agitated and have a recognised system for how and when the child accesses it.
7. If a child is coming into school feeling unsettled, have an adult 'meet and greet' for a few minutes, so they can be doing a calming activity before they access the classroom.
8. Have consistent approaches across home and school so that the child feels secure and supported, with everyone singing from the same song sheet.
9. Encourage all adults engaged with the child to remain calm and reasoned; anxiety from adults can easily affect how the child feels or behaves.
10. Look at suitable resources for managing anxiety in the form of programmes or games.

Case study 31

Child Y is struggling in class; he is disaffected from some aspects of the curriculum and often seems to 'daydream'. His teacher is concerned about him as he will say things out of context and can appear anxious about very small (to us) things. In my capacity as specialist teacher for SEMH I took him out for some one-to-one sessions to try to unpick what his anxieties were. He immediately told me about something he felt had 'gone wrong' for him a few months earlier and appeared to be 'reliving' how he felt on a regular basis. He then proceeded to tell me about a number of other issues affecting him (minor to us maybe but not to him) and these were clearly impacting on his ability to engage with learning and manage in social situations within school. There are some really useful books available on managing worries:

- *The Huge Bag of Worries* by Virginia Ironside (2011) is suitable for children aged five years upwards and is about Jenny, who finds she is being followed around by a huge blue bag full of worries, until a kind woman helps her so that the bag and the worries start to disappear.

- *When My Worries Get Too Big* by Kari Dunn Buron (2013), which is a relaxation book for children who live with anxiety.

I used the second book with Child Y; it has some great teaching activities to help a child self-manage their anxieties. These include a five-point scale that encourages a child to recognise their own emotions and identify triggers, and some calming-down strategies to 'bring them back down' if they become agitated. The child is encouraged to take ownership of what they feel helps them best and can share these with the adults around them. There is a helpful summary of the steps taken and Child Y took this home to share with his mum.

Before we worked through the book, I felt it was important to get rid of the 'baggage' Child Y had been carrying around for the past few months. Together we made a 'worry box' and posted into it all the things we had discussed; I then promised I would 'dispose' of the box on the understanding that he would stop worrying about things from the past that were no longer relevant. Child Y presented as having needs associated with ASC (I advised the school to support mum for a doctor's referral) and he took this very literally. On my next visit he declared that he no longer dwelled on these past worries and engaged well with the five-point scale, actively using it to describe how he was feeling. We decided that feeling '1' or '2' was desirable but that once he reached a '3' he needed to use his self-chosen calming strategies – deep breathing, going for a walk, accessing a calming safe space and writing stories. At '4' or '5' he was experiencing high levels of stress and needed adult support to 'bring him down', giving him time and space to calm. In subsequent sessions he was able to accurately assess his emotions using the scale and was beginning to self-regulate; he was able to say he often felt a '3' first thing on a Monday morning!

I am not suggesting as SENCO that you undertake this work with the children yourself, but you can be a facilitator and organise for a staff member or specialist to undertake the work. There are many online resources that can be used to support pupil wellbeing and, as stated in a previous chapter, www.mentallyhealthyschools.org.uk has a wealth of advice and support for primary schools. Obviously there may be outside influences impacting negatively on wellbeing, for example family circumstances, bereavement or trauma, and if so, other support services could be needed for the child or family. Again, it is about teamwork and being solution-focused; this has to be part of a whole-school approach.

Supporting parents

It is vital, as SENCO, that you give good support to the parents of your SEN pupils. When I was at the PRU, parents of excluded children often felt (rightly or wrongly) that they had been marginalised by their child's school due to the extent of their child's challenging behaviours and complex needs. In these circumstances, it is easy to get into a negative dialogue, playing the 'blame game', and relationships can then break down between school and home. It is natural for both schools and parents to adopt defensive positions in some situations, particularly if exclusion is a very real possibility, but it does not help the child if this happens. If we think about containment at these times, then there is often a lack of capacity to be calm, reasonable and properly reciprocal, so it is useful to think in advance about the qualities we need as SENCOs in supporting wellbeing and to try to uphold them. The parents I have spoken to over the years want a SENCO to:

- be approachable
- listen
- understand
- stay calm
- treat them with respect
- give of their time
- be non-judgemental and not condescending or argumentative
- be practical
- be solution-focused
- deliver on promises, e.g. making referrals
- be proactive – if something needs to be done, get it done; don't procrastinate or put things on the 'back burner' – no-one likes to be 'fobbed off'
- be clear and easily understood
- get the right help and support for the child
- work with class teachers and other staff to put in place an appropriate assess, plan, do, review

- keep them informed via phone calls and regular meetings
- give appropriate advice on next steps
- be honest – if you are not sure, do not 'fudge' issues and don't be afraid of saying you need to seek further advice.

Difficult situations that I have encountered have almost always been exacerbated when the above have not been adhered to. Parents of children with SEN are often desperate for help and reassurance and you are the 'face' of specialist support in school; you need to be reassuring and helpful and a person that can be trusted to do the right thing.

Case study 32

Child Q really struggled in the reception class and exhibited some really challenging behaviours; she had some support from the local PRU but it was clear that she had some unmet, complex needs. I referred her to a paediatrician in Year 1, with parental agreement, and eventually she was diagnosed with ADHD and trialled on medication. The school referred her for a placement in an alternative, nurturing provision whilst the meds were being monitored and strategies were transferred across on her return to school. I opened a CAF and TAF and paperwork was collated for an EHC needs assessment. This was accepted and Child Q received an EHCP. Key to this whole process was the relationship developed with parents, who were consulted and kept informed every step of the way. All actions were mutually agreed and this ultimately benefited the child, even when initially there was some parental hesitance over accessing the alternative provision (which worked really well).

There are a number of support groups for parents, for example https://youngminds.org.uk. It is useful if you can point parents in the direction of this support so that they get the right help. If a CAF or similar is open (or sometimes not, depending on your LEA) then early support services may be available as a commissioned resource for parents to access. There are a number of parenting initiatives, such as Incredible Years, which may be beneficial for parents (see www.incredibleyears.com for more information).

Supporting colleagues

When we looked at containment at the beginning of this chapter, we saw that 'overload' can easily occur if the person does not get proper supervision or support. Class teachers are expected to provide quality-first teaching for pupils with SEN and meet their individual needs regardless of any other adult support in class. They are expected to differentiate and provide individual programmes of work. If a child has complex underlying needs and challenging behaviours, this will be stressful for the child, the teacher and other children, so it is hardly surprising that teachers may struggle to cope. So, as SENCO, what can you do to help and support your colleagues?

The most important thing, in my opinion, is to show colleagues that you genuinely understand and care about them and their wellbeing. The child may be paramount but you cannot help the child if their teacher is poorly contained. I have known situations where teachers have approached their unions or gone off on long-term sick leave due to situations they have been forced to deal with outside of a supportive school network.

Class teachers are often very anxious about their children with SEN, particularly if they are struggling to meet their needs or if they display challenging behaviours. As SENCO, you can have a massive, positive effect on staff wellbeing if you are solution-focused and can give practical help and advice. If you have an SEN budget then you may be able to provide relevant resources that will keep the child calm, for example fidget toys or ear defenders. This can have a big impact on the wellbeing of all concerned if successful.

Case study 33

I have been supporting a child in a Key Stage 2 class who is at SEN support but whose family are reluctant for the child to engage with relevant professionals in assessing the child's special educational needs. The pupil is working significantly below age-related expectations but is keen to learn and is also very creative – she is brilliant at drawing and making things and loves taking part in class projects. She requires a lot of overlearning in core English and maths work and her class teacher is really struggling to foster some independence and scaffold future learning.

I was asked for help, which included consulting with the school specialist teacher, and came up with some solutions: simple maths games on the laptop that have a visual element, as she is engaged by images; a bank of high-interest sight words with visual cues; and some simple worksheets that reinforce basic skills and have a visual element (this is not the school norm but can be useful for children with SEN as an independent activity).

The teacher and teaching assistant put suggestions in place and these worked really well; the pupil was able to achieve some independence and her self-esteem was improved. The staff also felt empowered and were very happy that something was really working for the child! This has a knock-on effect on staff wellbeing because it takes away feelings of helplessness and means that something real and worthwhile is being achieved of which they have ownership.

I often go into the classrooms of my SEN pupils and observe or sit with them and then take them out for one-to-one interventions. This is useful for class teachers as I have first-hand experience of any issues and problems and can often offer further strategies to be tried. Recently, I have suggested putting in place an individual workstation for a child with recently diagnosed ADHD; this has reduced his ability to distract and be distracted and he now has a fidget toy (a stretchy person – these are great because they are cheap so it does not matter if they get broken; they come in big bags). He is much more settled and is able to get on with his work independently (he is working at age-related expectations). In the same class, I have suggested simple word banks, visual supports, and b and d reversal support cards, and have introduced Nessy Reading and Writing following Nessy dyslexic screening. This is now an established intervention in the class and is impacting positively on teaching and learning. Again, there is a positive effect on adult wellbeing because the interventions are working.

Top tip

If you cannot think of appropriate interventions, consult with nearby schools or your LEA SEND department for further advice and support.

Your educational psychologist should be able to help even if he or she cannot come out to look at the child.

Personal wellbeing

Your own positive wellbeing is vital as the demands of the SENCO role are huge at every level. So where can you get help? There are a number of websites and Twitter and Facebook pages that support adult wellbeing in schools. I am a member of a Twitter steering group, @HealthyToolkit, which promotes a number of initiatives such as #SelfCare; their latest mantra is 'Self-care is not selfish'. It is worth engaging with Twitter as there are so many supportive groups and individuals out there who promote brilliant ideas for wellbeing and SEND and give constructive SENCO support. The following is not an exhaustive list but may help you to get started:

- Sam at Schoolwell (@samschoolstuff, schoolwell.co.uk): Sam tweets about wellbeing opportunities and there is a wealth of resources on wellbeing on her website.
- Cherryl Drabble (@cherrylkd): Read her fantastic SEND book, *Bloomsbury CPD Library: Supporting Children with Special Educational Needs and Disabilities* (2016).
- #SENexchange: A wonderful SEN chat that covers a variety of SEND topics.
- SENCO Chat (@sencochat): They have a weekly chat on all things SENCO-related.
- Whole School Send (@WholeSchoolSend): Linked to NASEN SEND GATEWAY, sendgateway.org.uk/whole-school-send.
- IPSEA (@IPSEAcharity): They provide information about the law on SEND and parental support.
- Special Needs Jungle (@SpcialNdsJungle): They provide information about parental support and publish a wealth of articles that are really helpful and useful.

- ReachoutASC (www.reachoutasc.com and www.facebook.com/ReachoutASC): Run by a fabulous lady, Lynn McCann, who has a wealth of experience with ASC. She has three published books out with LDA, including: *How to Support Pupils with Autistic Spectrum Condition in Primary School* (2016) and *Stories That Explain: Social Stories for Children With Autism in Primary School* (2018) (both are available from www.amazon.co.uk).

As a SENCO, if you have access to a range of supportive networks, you are more likely to preserve your own health and wellbeing.

Things that may negatively impact your role

There are some factors to take into consideration when thinking about the effectiveness or otherwise of your SENCO role, which are best avoided or minimised as much as is practicable, and these are as follows:

- Combining the SENCO role with other significant teaching and management roles that impact on your SENCO time.
- Not having a secure base from which to work with proper storage (that is lockable).
- Not having secure practices and procedures in place to carry out the role effectively.
- Not having effective support from SLT (ideally you should be part of this, as per the SEND Code of Practice 2014).
- Not being part of a whole-school approach that places value on SEND and requires correct participation from all relevant personnel across the school.
- Not having an SEN budget to adequately meet the needs of SEN learners.
- Being asked by class teachers or senior leaders to put in place frameworks that are the preserve of quality-first teaching.
- Being asked to provide discrete assessment frameworks that are divorced from whole-school procedures.
- Being asked to implement procedures that are unlawful – see The Children and Families Act 2014 for more information.

- Being influenced by other school staff in how you help children and parents – this could include prejudices about particular pupils or certain parents; if this is not based on personal knowledge, avoid it (and if it is, you need to put personal views aside for the good of the children).
- Being asked to or expected to complete significant tasks in your own time.
- Being given insufficient SENCO time to do the job effectively.
- Being undermined by colleagues or SLT.
- Being expected to do something unreasonable by colleagues, SLT, teachers or parents.

It is important that your SENCO role is valued and validated and that all expectations are reasonable and can be managed in an expected time frame without causing stress. If you feel demands are unreasonable, you need to speak to a senior manager or headteacher to voice your concerns. Remember, the SENCO role is a statutory requirement within school and so is non-negotiable. Do not forget to enlist the help of your SEN governor as they can provide invaluable support in your role; they can also help you complete statutory tasks such as updating your SEN policy or updating the SEND part of the school website. Seek help and support from relevant professionals; as an independent practitioner, I am often called upon to support fellow professionals at a number of levels in school, but you may be able to access other support.

Chapter takeaways

- Ensure that all your systems are in place so that your role is effective.
- Correlate extra pieces of work to inform practice across the board.

Conclusion

So you are now an outstanding SENCO, with or without my pearls of wisdom, and you are using every strategy at your disposal to ensure that you are carrying out your role effectively and appropriately. You need to remember that no one is invincible and that you need as much support, both internally and externally, as possible to fulfil your obligations.

Please make sure that you consider your mental health needs, and those of others, in doing your job and legitimise this with your senior leadership team. I want to leave you with a checklist of best practice that you need to have in place in order to ensure you are fulfilling your role efficiently and effectively.

Check that:

- ☐ you have sufficient resources at your disposal to be effective and that you are able to support children and colleagues in the right way
- ☐ your actions are legally viable and in line with current legislation
- ☐ the needs of your pupils are being met through quality-first teaching with or without additional specialist support
- ☐ you have sufficient time to do the job effectively
- ☐ the strategies put in place are appropriate for the needs of the child
- ☐ assess, plan, do, review is in place and that small steps of progress are being measured
- ☐ there is quality-first teaching in place and that you are not doing the work of the classroom teacher
- ☐ parents are being appropriately advised and updated in line with their child's individual needs
- ☐ specialist support services are being used effectively, for example the specialist teacher

- ☐ you are working effectively with your county SEND department to facilitate correct provision for your children with SEND
- ☐ you are sufficiently upskilled in the various needs of your children with SEND and that the right strategies and support systems are in place; if not, ensure that you communicate with the right specialist support groups and individuals.

Finally, remember to be happy as well as efficient, as this will leave a lasting impact on your SEND children.

Good luck!

Glossary

ACEs: Adverse Childhood Experiences
ADHD: Attention Deficit Hyperactivity Disorder
APDR: Assess, Plan, Do, Review
ARE: Age-Related Expectations
ASC: Autistic Spectrum Conditions
CAF: Common Assessment Framework
CAMHS: Child and Adolescent Mental Health Services
CLA: Child Looked After
COP: Code of Practice for SEND
CYP: Child or Young Person
DfE: Department for Education
EHAs: Early Help Assessments
EHCP: Education Health and Care Plan – a statement of SEN for children and young people up to age 25
EP: Educational Psychologist
EYFS: Early Years Foundation Stage
HI: Hearing Impaired
IAS: Independent Advice and Support service for parents
IBP: Individual Behaviour Plan
IEP: Individual Education Plan
IPSEA: Independent Provider of Special Education Advice for parents
LEA: Local Education Authority
NAS: National Autistic Society
NGN: Nurture Group Network
Ofsted: Office for Standards in Education, Children's Services and Skills
OT: Occupational Therapist
PRU: Pupil Referral Unit
PSHE: Personal, Social and Health Education

SALT: Speech and Language Therapy

SEMH: Social, Emotional and Mental Health

SEN: Special Educational Needs, may also appear as SEND (Special Educational Needs and Disabilities)

SENCO: Special Educational Needs Co-Ordinator, may also appear as SENDCO (Special Educational Needs and Disabilities Co-Ordinator)

SEND Code of Practice 2014: A government document that covers the statutory requirements for SEND in schools and colleges

SLCN: Speech, Language and Communication Needs

SPD: Sensory Processing Disorder

SpLD: Specific Learning Difficulties

TA: Teaching Assistant

TAF: Team Around the Family

VI: Visually Impaired

References

ADHD Foundation (2012), 'FAQs', www.adhdfoundation.org.uk/faqs

Browning, K. (2015), 'Nasen Live 2015: high quality teaching', www.nasen.org.uk/utilities/download.0F820391-B9F5-435B-95C21072B953837F.html

Community Children's Health Partnership (2013), 'Community paediatricians referral', https://cchp.nhs.uk/cchp/clinicians/community-paediatricians-referral

Department for Education (2011), 'Teachers' standards', www.gov.uk/government/publications/teachers-standards

Department for Education (2012), 'SLCN pupils: how their needs change as they progress in school', www.gov.uk/government/publications/the-transitions-between-categories-of-special-educational-needs-of-pupils-with-speech-language-and-communication-needs-slcn-and-autism-spectrum-dis

Department for Education (2014a), 'SEND code of practice: 0 to 25 years', www.gov.uk/government/publications/send-code-of-practice-0-to-25

Department for Education (2014b), 'Young person's guide to the Children and Families Act 2014', www.gov.uk/government/publications/young-persons-guide-to-the-children-and-families-act-2014

Department for Education (2014c), 'SEND: guide for parents and carers', www.gov.uk/government/publications/send-guide-for-parents-and-carers

Drabble, C. (2016), *Bloomsbury CPD Library: Supporting Children with Special Educational Needs and Disabilities*. London: Bloomsbury Education.

Dunn Buron, K. (2013), *When My Worries Get Too Big!: A Relaxation Book for Children Who Live with Anxiety*. Shawnee, KS: AAPC Publishing.

Health Careers (2015a), 'Speech and language therapist', www.healthcareers.nhs.uk/explore-roles/allied-health-professionals/roles-allied-health-professions/speech-and-language-therapist

Health Careers (2015b), 'School nurse', www.healthcareers.nhs.uk/explore-roles/public-health/roles-public-health/school-nurse

IPSEA (2018), 'Asking for an EHC needs assessment', www.ipsea.org.uk/asking-for-an-ehc-needs-assessment

Ironside, V. (2011), *The Huge Bag of Worries*. London: Hodder Children's Books.

Lamb, B. (2018), 'Can OFSTED be a SENCO's best friend?', *Real Training*, https://realtraining.co.uk/2018/06/can-ofsted-be-a-sencos-best-friend
Kessler, Z. (2011), 'Class clown: why are ADHDers so damn funny?', https://blogs.psychcentral.com/adhd-zoe/2010/03/class-clown-why-are-adhders-so-damn-funny
McCann, L. (2016), *How to Support Pupils with Autism Spectrum Condition in Primary School*. Hyde: Learning Development Aids.
McCann, L. (2018), *Stories That Explain: Social Stories for Children With Autism in Primary School*. Hyde: Learning Development Aids.
McLeod, S. (2017), 'Bowlby's attachment theory', *Simply Psychology*, www.simplypsychology.org/bowlby.html
National Autistic Society (2016), 'Autism', www.autism.org.uk/about/what-is/asd.aspx
Nasen (2015), 'Resources', www.nasen.org.uk/resources
Nasen (2016), 'Supporting pupils with speech, language and communication needs', https://www.sendgateway.org.uk/r/supporting-children-with-speech-language-and-communication-needs-slcn_1.html
NHS (2014), 'Child and adolescent mental health services (CAMHS)', www.nhs.uk/using-the-nhs/nhs-services/mental-health-services/child-and-adolescent-mental-health-services-camhs
NHS (2018), 'Symptoms: attention deficit hyperactivity disorder (ADHD)', www.nhs.uk/conditions/attention-deficit-hyperactivity-disorder-adhd/symptoms
NHS Greater Glasgow and Clyde (2018), 'Paediatric occupational therapy within Greater Glasgow and Clyde', www.nhsggc.org.uk/kids/healthcare-professionals/paediatric-occupational-therapy
Ofsted (2015), 'School inspection handbook', www.gov.uk/government/publications/school-inspection-handbook-from-september-2015
The Communication Trust (2014), 'Working with speech and language therapists', www.thecommunicationtrust.org.uk/media/167275/s1_working_with_speech_and_language_therapists_final_jb.pdf
The School Run (2014), 'How can a clinical psychologist help your child with SEN?', www.theschoolrun.com/how-can-clinical-psychologist-help-your-child-sen
Tower Hamlets Council (2018), 'Information, Advice, and Support Services Network', www.localoffertowerhamlets.co.uk/organisations/28040-information-advice-and-support-services-network
UK Government (2014a), 'The Special Educational Needs and Disability Regulations 2014', www.legislation.gov.uk/uksi/2014/1530/contents/made
UK Government (2014b), 'Children and Families Act 2014', www.legislation.gov.uk/ukpga/2014/6/contents/enacted

Index